Italian
Conversation

Italian Conversation

Marcel Danesi

McGraw Hill

New York Chicago San Francisco Lisbon London Madrid Mexico City
Milan New Delhi San Juan Seoul Singapore Sydney Toronto

1 2 3 4 5 6 7 8 9 10 11 12 13 14 15 16 17   QDB/QDB   1 9 8 7 6 5 4 3 2

ISBN   978-0-07-177089-7
MHID   0-07-177089-5

e-ISBN   978-0-07-177090-3
e-MHID   0-07-177090-9

Library of Congress Control Number   2012931082

McGraw-Hill, the McGraw-Hill Publishing logo, Practice Makes Perfect, and related trade dress are trademarks or registered trademarks of The McGraw-Hill Companies and/or its affiliates in the United States and other countries and may not be used without written permission. All other trademarks are the property of their respective owners. The McGraw-Hill Companies is not associated with any product or vendor mentioned in this book.

Interior design by Village Bookworks, Inc.

McGraw-Hill products are available at special quantity discounts to use as premiums and sales promotions or for use in corporate training programs. To contact a representative, please e-mail us at bulksales@mcgraw-hill.com.

This book is printed on acid-free paper.

Contents

Preface

This book has one aim—to teach you how to converse in Italian and thus to get by in everyday situations. The emphasis is on how language is used in communication, not on the mechanics of the language in isolation, although there is plenty of that as well.

The book can be used by beginners, since nothing is taken for granted, or by those who have already been studying the language but would like to improve their conversation skills.

The book is made up of ten chapters. Each chapter revolves around a specific communication function and is subdivided into three themes. Each theme is constructed as follows:

- Two dialogues illustrate typical conversations related to the theme. English glosses are provided to enhance comprehension. This conversational material will help you to grasp how typical conversations are carried out in Italian. There are 60 dialogues in total, and reading these dialogues will enhance your conversation skills.
- Each dialogue is followed by a summary of the new vocabulary that it contains and a *Memory* section that allows you to check if you have learned important new words and structures.
- A *Language Notes* section explains and expands upon the grammatical and communicative material that the dialogue introduces.
- At the end of each thematic section there is an exercise section. This contains two types of activities—one that allows you to practice the new language forms and one that allows you to try out your conversation skills. There are thirty exercise sections in total, giving you ample practice!

A glossary of all the words and expressions used is provided at the end as well as an answer key to all exercises. Finally, there is an overall review section that allows you to test how much you have learned.

Here is a list of all abbreviations used in the book:

-a = corresponding feminine ending
ess. = conjugated with **essere** in compound tenses
f. = feminine
fam. = familiar, informal
inv. = invariable
isc = conjugated with **isc** in present tenses
m. = masculine
pl. = plural
pol. = polite, formal
sing. = singular

Pronunciation guide

Following are basic guidelines for pronouncing Italian words. Use these as you work your way through the book. Whenever a word that is difficult to pronounce comes up, its pronunciation will be given to you in parentheses.

Vowels

The Italian vowels are **a**, **e**, **i**, **o**, **u**. They are pronounced as follows:

LETTERS	PRONUNCIATION	AS IN . . .	EXAMPLES	MEANINGS
a	ah	*bah*	**ma**	*but*
e	eh	*bet*	**bene**	*well*
i	eeh	*beet*	**mio**	*my*
o	oh	*bought*	**ora**	*hour*
u	ooh	*boot*	**uno**	*one*

When **i** and **u** come before or after another vowel (in the same syllable), they are pronounced instead as follows:

LETTERS	PRONUNCIATION	AS IN . . .	EXAMPLES	MEANINGS
i	y	*yes*	**ieri**	*yesterday*
i	y	*say*	**sai**	*you know*
u	w	*way*	**uomo**	*man*
u	w	*cow*	**autista**	*driver*

Single consonants

Italian has both single and double consonants. Single consonants are pronounced as follows:

LETTERS	PRONUNCIATION	AS IN . . .	EXAMPLES	MEANING
b	b	*bat*	**bello**	*beautiful*
c (before a, o, u)	k	*cat*	**come**	*how*
ch (before e, i)			**chi**	*who*
c (before e, i)	ch	*chin*	**cinema**	*cinema*
ci (before a, o, u)			**ciao**	*hi/bye*
d	d	*dip*	**dentro**	*inside*

continued

LETTERS	PRONUNCIATION	AS IN . . .	EXAMPLES	MEANING
f	f	*fair*	**fare**	*to do*
g (before a, o, u) gh (before e, i)	g	*gas*	**gomma** **paghi**	*tire* *you pay*
g (before e, i) gi (before a, o, u)	j	*gym*	**gente** **giacca**	*people* *jacket*
gli	ly	*million*	**figlio**	*son*
gn	ny	*canyon*	**gnocchi**	*dumplings*
l	l	*love*	**latte**	*milk*
m	m	*man*	**madre**	*mother*
n	n	*name*	**nome**	*name*
p	p	*pen*	**pane**	*bread*
q	k(w)	*quick*	**qui**	*here*
r	r	*Brrrrr . . .*	**rosso**	*red*
s (unvoiced)	s	*sip* *spin*	**suo** **studente**	*his/her* *student*
s (voiced)	z	*zip*	**casa** **sbaglio**	*house* *mistake*
sc (before a, o, u) sch (before e, i)	sk	*skill*	**scuola** **fresche**	*school* *fresh (pl.)*
sc (before e, i) sci (before a, o, u)	sh	*shave*	**ascensore** **piscina**	*elevator* *pool*
t	t	*tent*	**tanto**	*a lot*
v	v	*vine*	**vero**	*true*
z	ts or ds	*cats or lads*	**zio**	*uncle*

Double consonants

Double consonants are not pronounced as such in English, even though there are double letters in the language. The Italian double consonants last approximately twice as long as corresponding single ones and are pronounced with more intensity. They occur between vowels or between a vowel and **l** or **r**.

EXAMPLES	MEANINGS
arrivederci	*good-bye*
bello	*beautiful*
caffè	*coffee*
camminare	*to walk*
formaggio	*cheese*
nonno	*grandfather*
occhio	*eye*

Spelling peculiarities

Generally, there is a one-to-one correspondence between a sound and the letter (or letters) used to represent it. The main exceptions are as follows:

- ◆ Words with a stressed final vowel are written with an accent mark on the vowel. The mark is usually grave. But in some, especially those ending in -**ché**, the acute accent mark may be used.

EXAMPLES	MEANINGS
caffè	*coffee*
città	*city*
perché	*why, because*
ventitré	*twenty-three*

- ◆ The letter **h** is used only in several present indicative tense forms of the verb **avere** *to have*. It is always silent.

EXAMPLES	MEANINGS
io ho	*I have*
tu hai	*you have* (fam.)
Lei ha	*you have* (pol.)
lui/lei ha	*he/she has*
loro hanno	*they have*

- ◆ As in English, capital letters are used at the beginning of sentences and to write proper nouns (names of people, countries, etc.). However, there are differences: the pronoun **io** (*I*), titles, months of the year, days of the week, and adjectives and nouns referring to languages and nationalities are not capitalized.

EXAMPLES	MEANINGS
dottore	*Dr.*
professore	*Professor*
signora	*Ms., Mrs.*
cinese	*Chinese*
inglese	*English*
italiano	*Italian*
gennaio	*January*
settembre	*September*
ottobre	*October*
lunedì	*Monday*
martedì	*Tuesday*

- ◆ On the other hand, the polite pronoun **Lei** (*you*), and other corresponding polite forms, are capitalized.

Making contact

Knowing how to make contact and to take leave of people is a vital conversational skill, as is knowing how to introduce people to each other and to ask for assistance. These are the topics of Italian conversation covered in this chapter.

Hellos and good-byes

Dialogo

Here's how two people, a man (**uomo**) and a woman (**donna**), might greet and take leave of each other formally:

UOMO: Buongiorno, signora Verdi.		*Good morning, Mrs. Verdi.*
DONNA: Buongiorno, signor Marchi.		*Good morning, Mr. Marchi.*
UOMO: Come va?		*How's it going?*
DONNA: Bene, grazie. E Lei?		*Well, thanks. And you?*
UOMO: Molto bene. Ci vediamo domani.		*Very well. See you tomorrow.*
DONNA: Sì, arrivederLa. A domani.		*Yes, good-bye. Till tomorrow.*

NEW VOCABULARY

a domani	see you tomorrow		**e**	and
arrivederLa	good-bye (*pol.*)		**grazie**	thank you
bene	well		**Lei**	you (*pol.*)
buongiorno	good morning, good day, hello		**molto**	very
ci vediamo	see you		**sì**	yes
come	how		**signora**	Mrs., madam, lady
Come va?	How's it going?		**signore**	Mr., sir, gentleman
domani	tomorrow		**uomo**	man
donna	woman			

Memory practice

After each new dialogue you will be given the opportunity to memorize important new forms with a simple fill-in-the-blanks exercise. Do this exercise from memory, and then go back and check your answers.

_____, signora Verdi.

Buongiorno, _____ Marchi.

Come va?

Bene, _____. E Lei?

_____ bene. Ci vediamo

_____.

Sì, _____. A domani.

Language notes

The expression **buongiorno** is used in the *morning* to greet and take leave of people, especially if they are on formal terms. In the *afternoon*, Italians now use **buon pomeriggio** and in the *evening*, **buonasera**. *Good night* is **buonanotte**. These can also be written as separate words: **buon giorno, buona sera, buona notte**.

Note that the complete form for *Mr.* or *sir* is **signore**. Before a name, however, the **-e** is dropped: **signor Marchi**. This applies to all masculine titles ending in **-e**. Note as well that the title is not capitalized, unless it is the first word in a sentence. Here are two other common titles used in conversations. Note that there is a different form for each gender.

MASCULINE TITLES	FEMININE TITLES
Professor	*Professor*
professore	professoressa
professor Bruni	professoressa Bruni
Dr.	*Dr.*
dottore	dottoressa
dottor Santucci	dottoressa Santucci

Dialogo

Here's how two friends—Giovanni, a young man, and Franca, a young woman—might greet and take leave of each other informally:

GIOVANNI: Ciao, Franca!	*Hi, Franca!*
FRANCA: Ah! Ciao, Giovanni!	*Ah! Hi, John!*
GIOVANNI: Come stai?	*How are you?*
FRANCA: Non c'è male. E tu?	*Not bad. And you?*
GIOVANNI: Benissimo, grazie!	*Very well, thanks!*
FRANCA: Ci vediamo presto, va bene?	*See you soon, OK?*
GIOVANNI: Certo. A presto. Ciao!	*Certainly. See you soon. Bye!*
FRANCA: Ciao!	*Bye!*

a presto	see you soon	**non**	not
benissimo	very well	**non c'è male**	not bad
certo	certainly, of course	**presto**	soon, early
ciao	hi, bye (*fam.*)	**stare**	to stay, to be
Come stai?	How are you? (*fam.*)	**tu**	you (*fam.*)
male	bad		

Memory practice

Fill in the blanks with the appropriate words and expressions. Do this from memory, and then go back and check your answers.

_____, Franca!

Ah! Ciao, Giovanni!

Come _____?

Non c'è male. E

_____?

_____, grazie!

Language notes

Italians address family, friends, children, pets, and anyone with whom they are on a first-name basis with familiar forms. Otherwise they would use formal or polite forms. Here are the relevant greeting forms according to level of formality:

FORMAL	INFORMAL
buongiorno, buon pomeriggio, buonasera	ciao [*the formal forms can also be used for informal speech if one is referring to actual time of day*]
Lei [*Note that it is always capitalized*]	tu
Come sta?	Come stai?
arrivederLa	ciao, arrivederci

Note the different pronouns (**Lei, tu**) and different verb forms (**sta, stai**) that reflect differences in formality.

ArrivederLa (written in this way!) is the polite form and **Arrivederci** the familiar one. **Ciao** can be used instead of **arrivederci**. And, as you have seen, **ciao** can mean both *hi* and *bye*.

Adding on -**issimo** to some words to mean *very* is common in Italian: **benissimo** (*very well*), **malissimo** (*very bad*).

Give the corresponding English or Italian word or expression.

ENGLISH	ITALIAN
1. man	_____
2. _____	signor Verdi
3. yes	_____
4. _____	professoressa Marchi
5. soon	_____
6. _____	dottor Bruni
7. and	_____
8. _____	professor Santucci
9. you (*pol.*)	_____
10. _____	signora Marchi
11. woman	_____
12. _____	dottoressa Santucci
13. of course	_____
14. _____	come
15. tomorrow	_____
16. _____	grazie
17. you (*fam.*)	_____
18. _____	molto
19. well	_____

Carry out the following conversation tasks.

20. Greet someone formally in the morning.

_____

21. Say good afternoon to someone politely.

_____

22. How would you say "See you tomorrow"?

_____

23. Say good-bye to someone formally.

_____

24. Say good-bye to a good friend.

_____

25. Ask someone "How's it going?"

_____

26. Say hi to a friend.

_____

27. Greet Mrs. Verdi in the morning.

_____

28. Greet Mr. Marchi in the evening.

_____

29. Greet Professor Santucci (a female) in the afternoon.

_____

30. Greet your friend Marcello.

_____

31. Say good night.

_____

Introductions

Dialogo

Here's how two strangers might introduce themselves to each other formally:

Uomo: Buonasera. Mi presento. Mi chiamo Tom Smith.	*Good evening. Allow me to introduce myself. My name is Tom Smith.*
Donna: Molto lieta! Mi presento anch'io. Mi chiamo Maria Morelli.	*Delighted! Allow me also to introduce myself. My name is Maria Morelli.*
Uomo: Molto lieto!	*Delighted!*
Donna: Lei è americano?	*Are you American?*
Uomo: Sì, sono americano. E Lei?	*Yes, I'm American. And you?*
Donna: Io sono italiana.	*I'm Italian.*
Uomo: Piacere di fare la Sua conoscenza.	*A pleasure to make your acquaintance.*
Donna: Anch'io.	*Me too.*

NEW VOCABULARY

americano	American	**lieto**	delighted
anche (anche io *or* **anch'io)**	also, too	**mi chiamo**	my name is

essere	to be	**mi presento**	let me introduce myself
io	I	**piacere di fare la**	a pleasure to make your
italiano	Italian	**Sua conoscenza**	acquaintance

Memory practice

Fill in the blanks with the appropriate words and expressions. Do this from memory, and then go back and check your answers.

Buonasera. Mi presento. Mi _____ Tom Smith.

Molto _____! Mi presento anch'io. Mi chiamo Maria Morelli.

_____ lieto!

Lei è _____?

Sì, sono americano. E Lei?

Io sono _____.

_____ di fare la Sua conoscenza.

Anch'io.

Language notes

You will have noticed that the ending on some words (nouns and adjectives) changes if the speaker (or the one spoken about) is a male or a female. If you are an American male you are **americano**; if you are an American female, then you are **americana**. More technically, regular forms ending in **-o** are masculine, those ending in **-a** are feminine. Note that there is no capitalization in Italian of nationalities (unless the word starts a sentence). Some nouns and adjectives end in **-e** (as you have seen). These may be either masculine or feminine.

MASCULINE	FEMININE
americano	americana
italiano	italiana
lieto	lieta
professore	professoressa
signore	signora
dottore	dottoressa

The expression **mi chiamo** (*My name is*) translates literally as *I call myself.*

In this and previous dialogues you have encountered a very important verb: **essere** (*to be*). Learn the forms below, which make up its conjugation in the present indicative. Note also that the pronouns (*I*, *you*, *he*, and so on) are optional in Italian when it is clear who the subject is: **io sono = sono**, **tu sei = sei**, and so on. Note also that **io** is not capitalized, unless it is the first word in a sentence.

(io) sono	*I am*
(tu) sei	*you are* (fam.)
(Lei) è	*you are* (pol.)
(lui) è	*he is*

(lei) è	*she is*
(noi) siamo	*we are*
(voi) siete	*you are* (pl.)
(loro) sono	*they are*

Dialogo

Here's how two young people might introduce themselves using an informal style of speech:

CLAUDIA: Come ti chiami?	*What's your name?*
BILL: Mi chiamo Bill Jones.	*My name is Bill Jones.*
CLAUDIA: Piacere!	*A pleasure!*
BILL: E tu?	*And you?*
CLAUDIA: Mi chiamo Claudia Santucci.	*My name is Claudia Santucci.*
BILL: Piacere di conoscerti! Sei italiana?	*A pleasure to know you! Are you Italian?*
CLAUDIA: Sì. E tu sei americano, vero?	*Yes. And you are American, right?*
BILL: Sì, sono americano.	*Yes, I'm American.*
CLAUDIA: Devo andare. A presto.	*I have to go. See you soon.*
BILL: Ciao, ciao.	*Bye-bye.*

NEW VOCABULARY

Come ti chiami?	What's your name?	**devo andare**	*I have to go*
piacere	a pleasure	**vero**	*true, right*
piacere di conoscerti (koh-nóh-sher-tee)	a pleasure to know you		

Memory practice

Fill in the blanks with the appropriate words and expressions. Do this from memory, and then go back and check your answers.

Come ti _____?

Mi _____ Bill Jones.

Piacere!

E tu?

Mi chiamo Claudia Santucci.

_____ di conoscerti! Sei italiana?

Sì. E tu sei americano, vero?

Sì, _____ americano.

Devo _____. A presto.

Ciao, ciao.

Language notes

Note a few more differences between formal and informal speech.

FORMAL	INFORMAL
Lei è (*you are*)	tu sei (*you are*)
Come si chiama (Lei)? (*What's your name?*)	Come ti chiami (tu)? (*What's your name?*)

**EXERCISE
1·2**

Circle the correct word or expression.

1. Mi presento. Mi chiamo Maria Rossini.

   Molto lieto.

   Anch'io.

2. E io mi chiamo Gina Dorelli.

   A presto.

   Piacere di fare la Sua conoscenza.

3. Maria è (*Maria is*) _____.

   italiano

   italiana

4. Tom è _____.

   americano

   americana

5. Io _____ americana.

   sono

   è

6. Anche tu _____ italiana, vero?

   siete

   sei

7. Anche Marco _____ italiano, vero?

   siamo

   è

Carry out the following conversation tasks.

8. Ask a stranger what his/her name is, using formal speech.

_____

9. Ask a little boy what his name is, using informal speech.

_____

10. Tell someone informally that you are glad to make his/her acquaintance.

_____

11. Say that you (yourself) are Italian.

_____

12. Say that you have to go.

_____

Assistance

Dialogo

Here's how someone might ask for assistance or directions in finding a place:

SIGNORINA:	Scusi, mi può aiutare?	_Excuse me, can you help me?_
SIGNORE:	Certo, signorina!	_Of course, Miss!_
SIGNORINA:	Dov'è via Nazionale?	_Where is National Street?_
SIGNORE:	Qui, a destra. È a due isolati.	_Here, to the right. It's two blocks away._
SIGNORINA:	Grazie.	_Thank you._
SIGNORE:	Non c'è problema!	_No problem!_

NEW VOCABULARY

a	at, to	**non**	not
a destra	to the right	**non c'è problema**	no problem
dove	where	**qui**	here
due	two	**scusi**	excuse me (_pol._)
isolato	block	**signorina**	Miss, Ms.
mi può aiutare	can you help me (_pol._)	**via**	street

Memory practice

Fill in the blanks with the appropriate words and expressions. Do this from memory, and then go back and check your answers.

_____, mi può aiutare?

Certo, _____!

_____ è via Nazionale?

Qui, a _____. È a due isolati.

Grazie.

Non c'è _____!

Language notes

Here are a few more differences between formal and informal speech:

FORMAL	INFORMAL
scusi	scusa
mi può aiutare	mi puoi aiutare

When asking for assistance, you will need to know the following question words.

che (cosa)	*what*
chi	*who*
come	*how*
dove	*where*
perché	*why*
Che (cosa) è?	*What is it?*
Chi è?	*Who is it?*
Come stai?	*How are you?*
Dov'è via Nazionale?	*Where's National Street?*
Perché non mi puoi aiutare?	*Why can't you help me?*

To ask a question that requires a yes/no response, all you have to do is put a question mark at the end (or raise your tone of voice if speaking). More commonly, do the same but put the subject at the end.

STATEMENT	QUESTION
Via Nazionale è qui a destra.	È qui a destra, via Nazionale?
National Street is here to the right.	*Is National Street here to the right?*
Maria è italiana.	È italiana, Maria?
Maria is Italian.	*Is Maria Italian?*

To make a verb negative, just put **non** before the verb.

AFFIRMATIVE	NEGATIVE
Via Nazionale è qui a destra.	Via Nazionale **non** è qui a destra.
National Street is here to the right.	*National Street is not here to the right.*
Maria è italiana.	Maria **non** è italiana.
Maria is Italian.	*Maria is not Italian.*

Note the following:

a destra   *to the right*   a sinistra   *to the left*

Finally, note that **isolati** (*blocks*) is the plural of **isolato** (*block*). In general, if the noun or adjective ends in **-o**, its plural form is obtained by changing it to **-i**.

SINGULAR	PLURAL
isolato (*block*)	isolati (*blocks*)
italiano (*Italian*)	italiani (*Italians*)
americano (*American*)	americani (*Americans*)
lieto (*delighted*)	lieti (*delighted*)

There are exceptions, of course. One of these is **uomo** (*man*) whose plural form is **uomini** (*men*).

Dialogo

Here's how one might ask for help in a bookstore:

CLIENTE:	Ho bisogno di un libro da leggere.	*I need a book to read.*
COMMESSO:	Le piacciono i romanzi d'avventura?	*Do you like adventure novels?*
CLIENTE:	Sì, molto. Perché?	*Yes, a lot. Why?*
COMMESSO:	Perché abbiamo un nuovo romanzo.	*Because we have a new novel.*
CLIENTE:	Dov'è?	*Where is it?*
UOMO:	In vetrina. Ecco il romanzo.	*In the window. Here's the novel.*
CLIENTE:	Mi piace molto.	*I like it a lot.*
CLIENTE:	Va bene.	*OK.*

NEW VOCABULARY

avventura	adventure	**molto**	a lot
cliente	customer	**nuovo**	new
commesso (-a)	clerk	**perché**	because
da leggere (léh-jjeh-reh)	to read	**piacere**	to like, to be pleasing to
di	of	**prendere (préhn-deh-reh)**	to take
ecco	here is	**romanzo**	novel
ho bisogno di	I need (I have need of)	**autore**	writer
in	in	**va bene**	OK
libro	book	**vetrina**	store window

Memory practice

Fill in the blanks with the appropriate words and expressions. Do this from memory, and then go back and check your answers.

Ho _____ di un libro da leggere.

Le _____ i romanzi d'avventura?

Sì, molto. Perché?

_____ abbiamo un nuovo romanzo.

Dov'è?

In vetrina. _____ il romanzo.

Mi _____ molto.

Va bene.

Language notes

In this dialogue you have come across another key verb: **avere** (*to have*). Here are its present indicative forms. Note that you do not pronounce the **h**. It is silent, as it is in English words such as *hour* and *honor*.

(io) ho	*I have*
(tu) hai	*you have* (fam.)
(Lei) ha	*you have* (pol.)
(lui) ha	*he has*
(lei) ha	*she has*
(noi) abbiamo	*we have*
(voi) avete	*you have* (pl.)
(loro) hanno	*they have*

In this dialogue, you have also come across your first articles in Italian. You will learn about them in bits and pieces. In front of a masculine noun beginning with a consonant (except **z** and **s** plus a consonant) or a vowel, the form for the *indefinite* article is **un**.

un libro	*a book*	un romanzo	*a novel*
un uomo	*a man*	un italiano	*an Italian*
un signore	*a gentleman*	un isolato	*a block*

The corresponding masculine *definite* article form is **il**. But it occurs only before consonants, other than **z** or **s** plus consonant. It does not occur before a vowel.

il libro	*the book*
il signore	*the gentleman*
il romanzo	*the novel*

The plural of **il** is **i**. And, as you know, to make a masculine noun plural, just change the **-o** (and **-e** for that matter) to **-i**.

i libri	*the books*
i signori	*the gentlemen*
i romanzi	*the novels*

For the time being, note that to say *I like*, you must use **mi piace** followed by a singular noun and **mi piacciono** (pyáh-choh-noh) followed by a plural noun.

SINGULAR	PLURAL
Mi piace il romanzo.	Mi piacciono i romanzi.
I like the novel.	*I like the novels.*
Mi piace il libro.	Mi piacciono i libri.
I like the book.	*I like the books.*

Finally, note that **perché** means both *why* and *because*.

EXERCISE 1·3

Do the following. Ask . . .

1. what it is

_____

2. who it is

_____

3. where the (male) clerk is

_____

4. your friend why he cannot help you

_____

Make each noun plural.

5. isolato _____

6. libro _____

7. italiano _____

8. romanzo _____

9. uomo (*be careful!*) _____

10. dottore _____

11. professore _____

Give the correct form of **avere**.

12. io _____

13. tu _____

14. il commesso _____

15. noi _____

16. voi _____

17. i commessi _____

Say that you like the following.

EXAMPLE: the book

Mi piace il libro.

18. the new novel

_____

19. the books

_____

20. the (male) doctor

21. the (male) professors

Carry out the following conversation tasks.

22. Say that you need a new book to read.

23. Ask someone politely if he/she likes adventure novels.

24. Say that the book is in the store window.

25. Say "Here is an adventure novel."

26. Say "OK."

27. Excuse yourself and ask a clerk if he/she can help you.

28. Now do the same, but this time you are speaking to a friend.

29. Say that National Street is here to the left, not to the right.

30. Say "Of course, Miss."

31. Say that it's two blocks away.

32. Say "no problem."

33. Say that Maria is not American.

34. Ask if Maria is Italian.

Numbers, time, dates

Knowing how to use numbers, how to tell the time, and how to ask for the date, among other basic notions, constitutes a critical conversational skill, wouldn't you agree? That's what this chapter is all about.

Numbers

Dialogo

Here's how someone might order at a café (**un bar**), using numerical concepts:

CLIENTE:	Vorrei un caffè espresso, per favore.	*I would like an espresso coffee, please.*
BARISTA:	Subito. Altro?	*Right away. Anything else?*
CLIENTE:	Sì, anche due o tre cornetti. Ho molta fame.	*Yes, also two or three croissants. I am very hungry.*
BARISTA:	Va bene. Altro?	*OK. Anything else?*
CLIENTE:	Sì, vorrei comprare dieci o undici panini da portare via. C'è una festa stasera a casa mia. Grazie.	*Yes, I would like to buy ten or eleven buns to take out. There's a party tonight at my house. Thanks.*
BARISTA:	Prego.	*You're welcome.*

NEW VOCABULARY

a casa mia	at my house	**da portare via**	to take out
altro	anything else, other	**espresso**	espresso
avere fame	to be hungry	**esserci**	to be there
bar	coffee place, bar	**festa**	party
barista	bartender	**panino**	bun sandwich
caffè	coffee	**per favore**	please
casa	house	**prego**	you're welcome
cliente	customer	**stasera**	tonight
comprare	to buy	**subito (sóoh-beeh-toh)**	right away
cornetto	croissant	**vorrei**	I would like

Memory practice

Fill in the blanks with the appropriate words and expressions. Do this from memory, and then go back and check your answers.

_____ un caffè espresso, per favore.

Subito. _____?

Sì, anche due o tre cornetti. Ho _____ fame.

Va bene. Altro?

Sì, vorrei _____ dieci o undici panini da portare via. C'è una _____ stasera a casa mia. Grazie.

Prego.

Language notes

The form **c'è** is from the verb **esserci**, which is really **essere** (as you know from the previous chapter), and **ci** (*there, here*). It is used to say *there/here is* (**c'è**) and *there/here are* (**ci sono**).

SINGULAR	PLURAL
C'è un bar qui.	**Ci sono** due bar qui.
There is a bar here.	*There are two bars here.*
Non **c'è** il barista.	Non **ci sono** i baristi.
The bartender is not here.	*The bartenders are not here.*

If you wish to point to something or someone, then **ecco** (which you came across in the previous chapter) is to be used.

C'è il barista?	Sì, **ecco** il barista.
Is the bartender here/there?	*Yes, there/here is the bartender.* (pointing him out)

Note that **caffè** ends with an accented vowel. This is rare in Italian. It means that the voice stress falls on that vowel. Also, note that the noun is masculine: **il caffè** (*the coffee*), **un caffè** (*a coffee*).

As used above, **molto** is an adjective. It agrees with the noun. This means that the ending changes according to the gender of the noun. For now, just notice that the masculine form of the adjective ends in **-o**, the feminine in **-a**. Note as well that the feminine form of the indefinite article is **una**, which is used before any consonant but not a vowel.

MASCULINE	FEMININE
molto caffè	molta fame
a lot of coffee	*very hungry* (= literally, *a lot of hunger*)
un nuovo libro	una nuova casa
a new book	*a new house*

The expression **avere fame** means, literally, "to have hunger": **Ho fame** = *I am hungry* ("I have hunger").

There were a few numbers used in the previous dialogue. Here are the first ten numbers in Italian:

1 uno	6 sei
2 due	7 sette
3 tre	8 otto
4 quattro	9 nove
5 cinque	10 dieci

Dialogo

Here's what someone might say when buying commemorative stamps, using numbers:

CLIENTE: Vorrei ventidue francobolli commemorativi, per favore.	*I would like twenty-two commemorative stamps.*
COMMESSA: Ecco i francobolli.	*Here are the stamps.*
CLIENTE: Quanto costano?	*How much do they cost?*
COMMESSA: Ogni francobollo costa trentacinque euro.	*Each stamp costs 35 euros.*
CLIENTE: Allora, ne prendo solo dieci.	*Then, I'll take only ten of them.*
COMMESSA: Belli, no?	*Beautiful, aren't they?*
CLIENTE: Molto.	*Very.*

NEW VOCABULARY

allora	then, thus	**ne prendo**	I'll take . . . of them
bello	beautiful	**no**	no
commemorativo	commemorative	**ogni**	each, every
costare	to cost	**quanto**	how much
euro	euro	**solo**	only
francobollo	stamp		

Memory practice

Fill in the blanks with the appropriate words and expressions. Do this from memory, and then go back and check your answers.

Vorrei ventidue francobolli _____, per favore.

Ecco i _____.

_____ costano?

Ogni francobollo _____ trentacinque euro.

Allora, ne prendo _____ dieci.

_____, no?

Molto.

Language notes

The numbers from 11 to 20 are as follows:

11 undici (óohn-dee-cheeh)	16 sedici (séh-deeh-cheeh)
12 dodici (dóh-deeh-cheeh)	17 diciassette (deeh-chahs-séh-teh)
13 tredici (tréh-deeh-cheeh)	18 diciotto (deeh-chóht-toh)
14 quattordici (kwáh-tohr-deeh-cheeh)	19 diciannove (deeh-chah-nóh-veh)
15 quindici (kwéehn-deeh-cheeh)	20 venti

Counting from twenty on is systematic. Just add on the numbers from one to ten to the twenties, thirties, etc., numerical part. If two vowels are involved in the combination, drop the first vowel. Here are the numbers from 21 to 29 fully constructed:

21 = venti + uno = ventuno (*Note the dropped vowel*)
22 = venti + due = ventidue
23 = venti + tre = ventitré (*Note the accent*)
24 = venti + quattro = ventiquattro
25 = venti + cinque = venticinque
26 = venti + sei = ventisei
27 = venti + sette = ventisette
28 = venti + otto = ventotto (*Note the dropped vowel*)
29 = venti + nove = ventinove

Here are the categories from 30 on:

30 trenta	200 duecento
40 quaranta	300 trecento
50 cinquanta	. . .
60 sessanta	1000 mille
70 settanta	2000 duemila (*Note the **mila** form in the plural*)
80 ottanta	3000 tremila
90 novanta	1.000.000 un milione
100 cento	2.000.000 due milioni

Note that the verb **costare** has a singular form, **costa** (*it costs*), and a plural form, **costano** (kóhs-tah-noh) (*they cost*).

SINGULAR	PLURAL
Il libro costa 30 euro.	I libri costano 300 euro.
The book costs 30 euros.	*The books cost 300 euros.*
Il panino costa molto.	I francobolli costano molto.
The bun costs a lot.	*The stamps cost a lot.*

Note that **molto** has various functions. Just remember that as an adjective it agrees with the noun, as you have seen.

The plural form **belli** is derived from the singular **bello** (*beautiful, handsome*). The feminine forms are **bella** (singular) and **belle** (plural). Note that the adjective follows the noun. This is a general principle, even though some adjectives can come before, as you will discover.

SINGULAR	PLURAL
un uomo bello	due uomini belli
a handsome man	*two handsome men*
una donna bella	due donne belle
a beautiful woman	*two beautiful women*

Finally, note that **euro** does not change in the plural: **un euro** (*a euro*), **due euro** (*two euros*).

EXERCISE
2·1

Make the entire phrase plural.

EXAMPLE: il caffè

i caffè (the coffees)

SINGULAR	PLURAL
1. il francobollo	_____
2. il cornetto	_____
3. il libro	_____
4. il panino	_____
5. il romanzo	_____

How do you say . . . ?

6. a house	_____
7. a new house	_____
8. a beautiful woman	_____
9. two euros	_____
10. three buns	_____
11. four novels	_____
12. five croissants	_____
13. six espressos	_____
14. seven men	_____
15. eight beautiful books	_____
16. nine euros	_____
17. ten commemorative stamps	_____
18. thirteen handsome men	_____
19. fourteen beautiful women	_____
20. fifteen beautiful houses	_____

21. sixteen, seventeen, eighteen   _____

22. nineteen, thirty-eight   _____

23. two hundred and fifty-three   _____

24. nine hundred and sixty-two   _____

25. two thousand and eighty   _____

Carry out the following conversation tasks.

26. Say you would like an espresso coffee, please.

_____

27. Ask someone if they would like something else.

_____

28. Say that you would like two or three croissants right away.

_____

29. Say that you are very hungry.

_____

30. Say, OK, you would like to buy two buns to take out.

_____

31. Say that there is a party at your house tonight.

_____

32. Give an appropriate answer when some says "**Grazie.**"

_____

33. Say that there is a new café-bar on (**in**) National Street.

_____

34. Say that there are no new books in the store window.

_____

35. Point to an espresso and indicate that it is there.

_____

36. Ask how much the stamps cost?

_____

37. Say that each bun costs eleven euros.

_____

38. Say: "Then, I'll take only twelve of them."

_____

Time

Dialogo

The following dialogue illustrates how one might ask what the time is:

MARIA: Giovanni, che ore sono?	*Giovanni, what time is it?*
GIOVANNI: È l'una e mezzo. No, è l'una e quarantacinque.	*It's half past one. No, it's one forty-five.*
MARIA: È tardi.	*It's late.*
GIOVANNI: Perché?	*Why?*
MARIA: Abbiamo un appuntamento col nostro professore.	*We have an appointment with our professor.*
GIOVANNI: A che ora?	*At what time?*
MARIA: Alle due.	*At two.*
GIOVANNI: Precise?	*Exactly?*
MARIA: Sì, alle due in punto.	*Yes, at two on the dot.*
GIOVANNI: Andiamo!	*Let's go!*

NEW VOCABULARY

andiamo	let's go	**mezzo**	half
appuntamento	appointment, date	**nostro**	our
Che ore sono?	What time is it?	**ora**	hour, time
con	with	**preciso**	precise (precisely)
in punto	on the dot	**tardi**	late

Memory practice

Fill in the blanks with the appropriate words and expressions. Do this from memory, and then go back and check your answers.

Giovanni, che _____ sono?

È l'una e _____. No, è _____ e quarantacinque.

È _____.

Perché?

Abbiamo un _____ col nostro professore.

A che _____?

_____ due.

Precise?

Sì, alle due in _____.

Andiamo!

Language notes

To ask for the time you can use either of the following formulas:

Che ora è? (literally: *What hour is it?*)   Che ore sono? (literally: *What hours are they?*)

To tell time, colloquially, all you have to do is count the hours, as in English, and add on the minutes. For one o'clock the verb is singular (**è**), while for the other hours it is plural (**sono**). Here are a few examples:

È l'una.	*It's one o'clock.*
Sono le due e dieci.	*It's two ten.*
Sono le cinque e venti.	*It's five twenty.*

Note that the form **alle** is a contracted form: **a + le = alle**. For one o'clock it is **a + l' = all'**. By the way, you have just come across another form of the definite article, namely, **l'**, which is used before nouns beginning with vowels: **l'appuntamento** (*the appointment*), **l'ora** (*the hour*), **l'avventura** (*the adventure*).

All'una.	*At one o'clock.*
Alle due e dieci.	*At two ten.*
Alle cinque e venti.	*At five twenty.*

Note that **un quarto** means *a quarter*, and **mezzo** *half*. Note also that to distinguish the morning hours from the afternoon and evening ones, you can use **della mattina** (*in the morning*), **del pomeriggio** (*in the afternoon*), and **della sera** (*in the evening*), respectively. Note that the forms **del** and **della** are contractions: **d + il = del, di + la = della**.

Sono le sette e un quarto.	*It's a quarter past seven.*
Alle undici e mezzo.	*At half past eleven.*
Sono le otto e quaranta della mattina.	*It's eight forty a.m.*
Alle nove e venticinque della sera.	*At nine twenty-five p.m.*
Sono le tre e tredici del pomeriggio.	*It's three thirteen in the afternoon.*

By the way, the word for *noon* is **mezzogiorno**, and the word for *midnight* is **mezzanotte**: **È mezzogiorno** (*It's noon*); **È mezzanotte** (*It's midnight*).

Notice that **preciso** is an adjective agreeing with **ore**. That's why its form is **precise**.

Finally, note that **col professore** is again a contracted form: **con + il**. You will learn more about such forms in due course.

Dialogo

Here's the kind of brief conversation someone might have with a tour guide involving times of the day and night:

GUIDA:	Il giro comincia oggi alle sedici e quaranta.	*The tour begins today at four forty.*
TURISTA:	Quando finisce?	*When does it end?*
GUIDA:	Alle diciotto circa.	*At around six.*
TURISTA:	Troppo tardi! Ho un appuntamento alle venti.	*Too late! I have an appointment at eight.*

GUIDA: C'è un giro anche domani alla stessa ora. *There's a tour tomorrow, too, at the same time.*

TURISTA: Allora, torno domani. *Then, I'll be back tomorrow.*

NEW VOCABULARY			
circa	around, nearly	**oggi**	today
cominciare	to begin, to start	**quando**	when
domani	tomorrow	**stesso**	same
finire	to finish	**tornare**	to return, to come back
giro	tour	**troppo**	too, too much
guida	guide	**turista**	tourist (*male or female*)

Memory practice

Fill in the blanks with the appropriate words and expressions. Do this from memory, and then go back and check your answers.

Il giro _____ oggi alle sedici e quaranta.

_____ finisce?

Alle _____ circa.

_____ tardi! Ho un appuntamento alle venti.

C'è un giro anche domani alla _____ ora.

Allora, _____ domani.

Language notes

In Italy, the tendency is to use the twenty-four-hour clock. This is certainly the case for schedules of any kind (bus, train, TV, etc.). So, after twelve noon, you just continue counting to twenty-four.

Sono le quattordici e trenta.	*It's two thirty (afternoon).*
Sono le diciannove.	*It's seven (evening).*
Sono le ventitré e dieci.	*It's eleven ten (evening).*

Note that **alla** is a contraction of **a + la** and that **stesso** is an adjective that agrees with the noun: **alla stessa ora** (*at the same hour*).

You have encountered three verb forms in the present indicative in this dialogue—**comincia**, **finisce**, and **torno**. We will deal with verbs like **finisce** later. The other two verbs are present indicative forms of **cominciare** (*to begin*) and **tornare** (*to return, to come back*). To conjugate verbs such as these, called first-conjugation verbs ending in **-are**, drop the **-are** ending and add the following endings according to person. Here's **tornare** fully conjugated:

(io) torn**o**	*I return, am returning*
(tu) torn**i**	*you return, are returning (fam.)*
(Lei) torn**a**	*you return, are returning (pol.)*
(lui) torn**a**	*he returns, is returning*
(lei) torn**a**	*she returns, is returning*

(noi) torn**iamo**	*we return, are returning*
(voi) torn**ate**	*you return, are returning* (pl.)
(loro) torn**ano** (tóhr-nah-noh)	*they return, are returning*

In the case of verbs like **cominciare**, which end in **-ciare**, do not keep the **-i** in front of another **-i**: **io comincio, tu cominci, Lei comincia, noi cominciamo, voi cominciate, loro cominciano.**

EXERCISE

2·2

Give the indicated times following the example.

EXAMPLE: 2:25 (P.M.)

Sono le due e venticinque del pomeriggio./Sono le quattordicie venticinque.

1. 1:10 (P.M.) _____

2. 3:30 (P.M.) _____

3. 4:12 (P.M.) _____

4. 9:10 (A.M.) _____

5. 10:15 (A.M.) _____

6. 7:35 (P.M.) _____

7. 9:48 (P.M.) _____

8. noon _____

9. midnight _____

Say that the indicated person is coming back or starting something at the given time. Use only official time. Follow the examples.

EXAMPLES: Maria/tornare/2:25 (P.M.)

Maria torna alle quattordici e venticinque.

Io/cominciare/6:30 (A.M.)

Io comincio alle sei e trenta/mezzo.

10. tu/tornare/7:15 (P.M.) _____

11. la donna/cominciare/8:38 (A.M.)

_____

12. noi/cominciare/10:30 (A.M.) _____

13. voi/tornare/10:20 (P.M.) _____

14. loro/cominciare/11:10 (A.M.) _____

15. io/cominciare/1:05 (P.M.) _____

Carry out the following conversation tasks.

16. Ask someone what time it is.

_____

17. Tell someone that, no, it's not late.

_____

18. Say that you have an appointment at precisely 4 P.M. with the professor.

_____

19. Say that Maria is coming back at 8 P.M. on the dot.

_____

20. Ask when something is finishing.

_____

21. Say that it is finishing at around ten in the evening.

_____

22. Say that the tour is beginning too late.

_____

23. Ask if there is a tour that (**che**) begins at (**a**) noon?

_____

24. Say that, then, you are coming back tomorrow at the same hour.

_____

Dates

Dialogo

Here's a typical conversation that might unfold between friends discussing dates and birthdays:

MARCO: Dina, quanti ne abbiamo oggi?	*Dina, what's today's date?* (literally: *How many of them* [days] *do we have?*)
DINA: Oggi è il due novembre.	*It's November 2.*
MARCO: Allora, se non sbaglio, è il tuo compleanno?	*Then, if I'm not mistaken, it's your birthday?*
DINA: Sì.	*Yes.*
MARCO: Buon compleanno! Quanti anni hai?	*Happy birthday! How old are you?*
DINA: Ho ventitré anni.	*I'm twenty-three years old.*
MARCO: Sembri ancora una bambina!	*You still look like a little girl!*

ancora	still, yet	**compleanno**	birthday
anno	year	**sbagliare**	to make a mistake
avere… anni	to be…old	**se**	if
bambino/bambina	little boy/girl, child	**sembrare**	to seem
Buon compleanno!	Happy birthday!	**tuo**	your (*fam.*)

Memory practice

Fill in the blanks with the appropriate words and expressions. Do this from memory, and then go back and check your answers.

Dina, _____ ne abbiamo oggi?

Oggi è _____ due novembre.

Allora, se non _____, è il tuo compleanno?

Sì.

_____ compleanno! Quanti anni hai?

_____ ventitré anni.

Sembri _____ una bambina!

Language notes

Note that **quanto** can function as an adjective, agreeing with the noun of course. We will discuss adjectives more completely later. Note again the difference between familiar and polite speech.

Quant**i** anni hai? (*fam.*)	*How old are you?*
Quant**i** anni ha? (*pol.*)	*How old are you?*
Quant**o** caffè prendi?	*How much coffee are you having?*
Quant**e** case nuove ci sono?	*How many new houses are there?*

Note the expression **quanti ne abbiamo**, which means, literally, *how many of them* (days) *do we have*?

Also note that to indicate age, Italian uses the expression **avere… anni**, meaning, literally, *to have . . . years*.

Ho trentadue anni.	*I am thirty-two years old.* (literally: *I have thirty-two years.*)
La bambina ha dieci anni.	*The little girl is ten years old.* (literally: *The little girl has ten years.*)

To talk about birthdays, you'll need to know the months of the year. Here they are:

gennaio	*January*	luglio	*July*
febbraio	*February*	agosto	*August*
marzo	*March*	settembre	*September*
aprile	*April*	ottobre	*October*
maggio	*May*	novembre	*November*
giugno	*June*	dicembre	*December*

Here's how to indicate dates. Note that the definite article is used and that the number precedes the month.

il quattro luglio	*July 4*
il dieci agosto	*August 10*
il tre maggio	*May 3*
il venticinque dicembre	*December 25*
l'otto marzo	*March 8*
il primo luglio	*July 1*

Be careful with the eighth day of the month. It starts with a vowel, so the appropriate form of the article is **l'otto**. Note also that for the first day of each month you must use the ordinal number **primo**: **il primo luglio**.

Dialogo

Here's a conversation between a husband and wife involving dates:

MARITO:	Che giorno è, cara?	*What day is it, dear?*
MOGLIE:	Lunedì.	*Monday.*
MARITO:	È terribile! Dimentico sempre tutto!	*It's terrible. I always forget everything.*
MOGLIE:	Ma ricordi in che anno sono nata, no?	*But you do remember the year in which I was born, don't you?*
MARITO:	Sì. Nel 1985 (mille novecento ottantacinque).	*Yes, in 1985.*
MOGLIE:	Meno male!	*Thank goodness!*

NEW VOCABULARY

caro (-a)	dear		**moglie**	wife
dimenticare	to forget		**ricordare**	to remember
essere nato (-a)	to be born		**sempre**	always
ma	but		**terribile**	terrible
marito	husband		**tutto**	everything
Meno male!	Thank goodness!			

Memory practice

Fill in the blanks with the appropriate words and expressions. Do this from memory, and then go back and check your answers.

Che _____ è, cara?

Lunedì.

È terribile! Dimentico _____ tutto!

Ma _____ in che anno sono _____, no?

Sì. _____ 1985 (mille novecento ottantacinque).

_____!

Language notes

Knowing the days of the week is essential to many conversations.

lunedì	*Monday*
martedì	*Tuesday*
mercoledì	*Wednesday*
giovedì	*Thursday*
venerdì	*Friday*
sabato (sáh-bah-toh)	*Saturday*
domenica (doh-méh-neeh-kah)	*Sunday*

Note that **nel** is a contraction of **in + il**. Note also that the year is preceded by the article or the contracted article as follows:

> **il** mille novecento novantaquattro (1994)
>
> **nel** duemila sette (*in 2007*)

Note the expression **essere nato** (**-a**), which varies according to gender.

(Io) sono nato (-a) nel 1992.	*I was born in 1992.*
Marco è nato nel 1989.	*Marco was born in 1989.*
Maria è nata nel 2000.	*Maria è nata nel duemila.*

Finally, note that in conjugating the verb **dimenticare** in the present indicative, you have to add an **h** before the **i** ending to retain the hard sound of the **c**.

(io) dimentico	*I forget*

But:

(tu) dimentichi (deeh-méhn-teeh-keeh)	*you forget*
(noi) dimentichiamo	*we forget*

EXERCISE 2·3

Using a complete sentence, give the following dates.

EXAMPLE: Friday, October 12

Oggi è venerdì, il dodici ottobre.

1. Monday, January 1

_____

2. Tuesday, February 8

_____

3. Wednesday, March 10

_____

4. Thursday, April 12

_____

5. Friday, May 28

_____

6. Saturday, June 23

_____

7. Sunday, July 4

_____

Put the correct form of **quanto** *in front of the following nouns.*

8. _____ anni hai, Maria?

9. _____ euro ha, signor Marchi?

10. _____ caffè prendi, Marco?

11. _____ donne ci sono qui?

Say that the following were born in the indicated year.

EXAMPLE: Sara/1998

         Sara è nata nel 1998.

12. Alessandro/1994

_____

13. la moglie/1987

_____

14. il marito/1984

_____

Carry out the following conversation tasks.

15. Ask someone what today's date is.

_____

16. Say that, if you are not mistaken, it is Maria's birthday (**il compleanno di Maria**).

_____

17. Wish someone a happy birthday.

_____

18. Ask a friend how old he/she is.

_____

19. Ask someone formally how old he/she is.

_____

20. Say that you are thirty-six years old.

_____

21. Tell a friend that he still looks like a little boy.

_____

22. Ask someone what day it is.

_____

23. Say that it's terrible.

_____

24. Say that the husband always forgets everything.

_____

25. Say "But we, too, always forget everything."

_____

26. Say that you remember the year in which someone was born.

_____

Getting information

Needless to say, knowing how to get the information you might need, to ask for directions, or simply to chat on the phone or to text someone, constitutes an important ability in everyday life. This chapter shows you how to acquire this skill in Italian.

Information

Dialogo

Here's what a conversation between two friends who haven't seen each other for a while might sound like, especially if they want to catch up on things:

FRANCA:	Maria, dove abiti adesso?	*Maria, where do you live now?*
MARIA:	Qui a Bari. E tu, Franca?	*Here in Bari. And you, Franca?*
FRANCA:	Anch'io abito a Bari.	*I also live in Bari.*
MARIA:	Dove?	*Where?*
FRANCA:	In via Dante.	*On Dante Street.*
MARIA:	Io abito molto vicino a te, in via Machiavelli.	*I live very near you, on Machiavelli Street.*
FRANCA:	Ottimo! Qualcuno mi ha detto che sei sposata. È vero?	*Excellent! Someone told me that you are married. Is it true?*
MARIA:	No. E tu?	*No. And you?*
FRANCA:	Non ancora. Mi piace la libertà, per adesso!	*Not yet. I like freedom, for now.*

NEW VOCABULARY
---

abitare	to live, to dwell	**ottimo (óh-teeh-moh)**	excellent
adesso	now	**per**	for, through
che	that, which, who	**qualcuno**	someone
essere sposato (-a)	to be married	**vicino**	near

Memory practice

Fill in the blanks with the appropriate words and expressions. Do this from memory, and then go back and check your answers.

Maria, dove abiti _____?

Qui _____ Bari. E tu, Franca?

Anch'io _____ a Bari.

Dove?

_____ via Dante.

Io abito molto _____ a te, in via Machiavelli.

Ottimo! Qualcuno mi ha detto che sei _____. È vero?

No. E tu?

Non ancora. Mi piace la _____, per adesso!

Language notes

To say *in + city* use **a + città**; to say *in + country*, use **in + paese**.

a Bari	*in Bari*
a Roma	*in Rome*
a Firenze	*in Florence*
in Italia	*in Italy*
in Francia	*in France*

Note that *in the United States* is **negli Stati Uniti**. The reason is that *United States* is in the plural.

In this conversation, for now just note that **ha detto** is a past tense. We will deal with this tense later on.

Note, also, that **che** is a relative pronoun in the dialogue. In this function it means *that, which, who*.

La donna **che** abita a Bari si chiama Maria.	*The name of the woman who lives in Bari is Maria.*
Il libro **che** vorrei comprare è molto bello.	*The book that I would like to buy is very beautiful.*

Dialogo

Now, here's a similar conversation to the previous one. Again, two friends are chatting and catching up on things.

VANESSA: Gina! Come stai? E come sta tuo fratello che non vedo da molto?	*Gina! How are you? And how is your brother whom I haven't seen for a while?*
GINA: Tutti bene. È sposato, sai? E ha bambini.	*All (of us) well. He's married, you know? And he has children.*
VANESSA: Che bello! Quanti?	*How nice! How many?*
GINA: Tre.	*Three.*
VANESSA: Dove abita adesso?	*Where does he live now?*
GINA: A Perugia. Ma viene spesso qui.	*In Perugia. But he comes here often.*
VANESSA: Quando verrà la prossima volta?	*When will he be coming next time?*
GINA: Non sono sicura.	*I'm not sure.*

da	from (for)	**stare**	to stay, to be
fratello	brother	**tutti**	everyone
prossimo (próhs-seeh-moh)	next	**vedere**	to see
sapere	to know	**venire**	to come
sicuro	sure	**verrà**	he/she will come
spesso	often	**volta**	time (occurrence)

Memory practice

Fill in the blanks with the appropriate words and expressions. Do this from memory, and then go back and check your answers.

Gina! Come stai? E come _____ tuo fratello che non vedo da molto?

_____ bene. È sposato, sai? E ha bambini.

Che bello! Quanti?

Tre.

Dove abita _____?

A Perugia. Ma _____ spesso qui.

Quando verrà la _____ volta?

Non sono _____.

Language notes

You've come across the verb **stare** a few times already. It is used to ask how someone is, although it really means *to stay*. It is an irregular verb (like **essere** and **avere**). Here is its conjugation in the present indicative:

(io) sto	*I am, stay*
(tu) stai	*you are, stay* (fam.)
(Lei) sta	*you are, stay* (pol.)
(lui) sta	*he is, stays*
(lei) sta	*she is, stays*
(noi) stiamo	*we are, stay*
(voi) state	*you are, stay* (pl.)
(loro) stanno	*they are, stay*

The dialogue contains two other irregular verbs (that is, verbs whose forms are not derived systematically)—**venire** and **sapere**. Needless to say, they are important verbs if you want to converse in Italian. Here are their present indicative forms:

venire (*to come*)	
(io) vengo	*I come, I am coming*
(tu) vieni	*you come, you are coming* (fam.)
(Lei) viene	*you come, you are coming* (pol.)

(lui) viene	*he comes, he is coming*
(lei) viene	*she comes, she is coming*
(noi) veniamo	*we come, we are coming*
(voi) venite	*you come, you are coming* (pl.)
(loro) vengono (véhn-goh-noh)	*they come, they are coming*

sapere (*to know*)

(io) so	*I know*
(tu) sai	*you know* (fam.)
(Lei) sa	*you know* (pol.)
(lui) sa	*he knows*
(lei) sa	*she knows*
(noi) sappiamo	*we know*
(voi) sapete	*you know* (pl.)
(loro) sanno	*they know*

Previously you have come across a different kind of *knowing*—*knowing* or *meeting someone*. The verb was **conoscere**. It is a regular verb of the second conjugation—namely, verbs ending in -**ere**. To conjugate such verbs, drop the -**ere** and add the following endings:

(io) conosc**o**	*I know*
(tu) consosc**i**	*you know* (fam.)
(Lei) conosc**e**	*you know* (pol.)
(lui) conosc**e**	*he knows*
(lei) conosc**e**	*she knows*
(noi) conosc**iamo**	*we know*
(voi) conosc**ete**	*you know* (pl.)
(loro) conosc**ono** (koh-nóhs-koh-noh)	*they know*

In the dialogue, you have come across another second-conjugation verb—**vedere**; and in a previous chapter, **prendere** (*to take*) and **leggere** (*to read*). These are conjugated with the same endings.

It is time to summarize the system of regular nouns, before we proceed. As you know by now, if the noun ends in -**o** it is normally masculine; to form its plural, change the -**o** to -**i**. If the noun ends in -**a** it is usually feminine; to form its plural change the -**a** to -**e**.

SINGULAR	PLURAL
Masculine	
anno (*year*)	anni (*years*)
francobollo (*stamp*)	francobolli (*stamps*)
Feminine	
donna (*woman*)	donne (*women*)
casa (*house*)	case (*houses*)

Nouns ending in -**e** can be either masculine or feminine (you will have to look this up if you are unsure). In either case, the plural is formed by changing the -**e** to –**i**.

SINGULAR	PLURAL
Masculine	
professore (*professor*)	professori (*professors*)
dottore (*doctor*)	dottori (*doctors*)
Feminine	
moglie (*wife*)	mogli (*wives*)
madre (*mother*)	madri (*mothers*)

EXERCISE
3·1

Put the following nouns into their plural forms.

1. americano _____

2. appuntamento _____

3. avventura _____

4. bambino _____

5. bambina _____

6. dottoressa _____

7. romanzo _____

8. sera _____

9. moglie _____

10. dottore _____

Ask how the following people are.

EXAMPLE: tu

             Come stai (tu)?

11. tuo fratello _____

12. voi _____

13. Lei _____

14. i bambini _____

Give the corresponding forms of each verb according to person.

	VENIRE	SAPERE	CONOSCERE
15. io	_____	_____	_____
16. tu	_____	_____	_____
17. lui/lei	_____	_____	_____
18. noi	_____	_____	_____

19. voi   _____   _____   _____

20. loro   _____   _____   _____

Carry out the following conversation tasks.

21. Ask a friend where he/she is living now.

   _____

22. Ask Mrs. Marchi where she is living now. (*Don't forget to use the polite form of the verb.*)

   _____

23. Say that you live in Florence.

   _____

24. Say that Mrs. Marchi (**la signora Marchi**) lives in Italy. (*Note the use of the article with a title when talking about someone.*)

   _____

25. Say that Mr. Verdi (**il signor Verdi**) lives on Dante Street.

   _____

26. Say that you live near Maria.

   _____

27. Say that you live in the United States.

   _____

28. Say that someone said that you are married.

   _____

29. Say that, for now, you like freedom.

   _____

30. Say that the novel you are reading is new.

   _____

31. Ask a friend how his/her brother is.

   _____

32. Say that he is married and has children.

   _____

33. Say that you are not sure when he will be coming the next time.

   _____

34. Say that he comes often to Rome.

   _____

35. Say that you know how to read in Italian (**italiano**).

   _____

36. Say that you do not know the professor of Italian (**d'italiano**).

_____

Directions

Dialogo

Here's how someone might ask for directions:

SIGNORE: Scusi, mi sa dire dov'è via Dante?   _Excuse me, can you tell me where Dante Street is?_

SIGNORINA: Certo! Vada a sinistra per due isolati.   _Certainly. Go left for two blocks._

SIGNORE: E poi?   _And then?_

SIGNORINA: Giri a destra al semaforo.   _Turn right at the traffic lights._

SIGNORE: Devo attraversare la strada?   _Should I cross the street?_

SIGNORINA: Sì, e vada diritto per ancora due isolati.   _Yes, and go straight ahead for two more blocks._

SIGNORE: Lì, c'è via Dante?   _Is Dante Street there?_

SIGNORINA: Sì.   _Yes._

NEW VOCABULARY

andare	to go	**girare**	to turn
attraversare	to cross	**lì**	there
dire	to tell, to say	**poi**	then
diritto	straight ahead	**semaforo (seh-máh-foh-roh)**	traffic lights
dovere	to have to, must	**strada**	road, street

Memory practice

Fill in the blanks with the appropriate words and expressions. Do this from memory, and then go back and check your answers.

Scusi, mi sa _____ dov'è via Dante?

Certo! _____ a sinistra per due isolati.

E _____?

Giri a destra al _____.

_____ attraversare la strada?

Sì, e vada _____ per ancora due isolati.

_____, c'è via Dante?

Sì.

Language notes

This dialogue introduces you to three new and very useful verbs. Here are their conjugations in the present indicative:

dovere (*to have to, must*)

(io) devo	*I have to, I must*
(tu) devi	*you have to, you must* (fam.)
(Lei) deve	*you have to, you must* (pol.)
(lui) deve	*he has to, he must*
(lei) deve	*she has to, she must*
(noi) dobbiamo	*we have to, we must*
(voi) dovete	*you have to, you must* (pl.)
(loro) devono (déh-voh-noh)	*they have to, they must*

dire (*to tell, to say*)

(io) dico	*I say, I am saying*
(tu) dici	*you say, you are saying* (fam.)
(Lei) dice	*you say, you are saying* (pol.)
(lui) dice	*he says, he is saying*
(lei) dice	*she says, she is saying*
(noi) diciamo	*we say, we are saying*
(voi) dite	*you say, you are saying* (pl.)
(loro) dicono (déeh-koh-noh)	*they say, they are saying*

andare (*to go*)

(io) vado	*I go, I am going*
(tu) vai	*you go, you are going* (fam.)
(Lei) va	*you go, you are going* (pol.)
(lui) va	*he goes, he is going*
(lei) va	*she goes, she is going*
(noi) andiamo	*we go, we are going*
(voi) andate	*you go, you are going* (pl.)
(loro) vanno	*they go, they are going*

The forms **vada** and **giri** are imperative forms. Just note this for now. The form **al** is a contraction of **a + il**. We will complete the discussion of contractions in the next chapter. Now it is time to summarize both the forms of the indefinite article and the forms of adjectives.

The indefinite article has the following forms:

- **uno** before a masculine noun (or adjective) beginning with **z** or **s** + consonant: **uno zio** (*an uncle*), **uno studente** (*a student*)
- **un** before all other masculine nouns (or adjectives): **un bambino** (*a little boy*), **un uomo** (*a man*)
- **una** before feminine nouns beginning with any consonant: **una zia** (*an aunt*), **una studentessa** (*a female student*)
- **un'** before feminine nouns beginning with any vowel: **un'americana** (*an American woman*), **un'avventura** (*an adventure*)

Adjectives end in **-o** or **-e**: **alto** (*tall*), **grande** (*big*). The ending changes according to the noun, as you have seen several times. Most adjectives are placed after the noun. Here are all the possibilities:

SINGULAR	PLURAL
Masculine	
il bambino alt**o**	i bambini alt**i**
the tall boy	*the tall boys*
il padre alt**o**	i padri alt**i**
the tall father	*the tall fathers*
il bambino grand**e**	i bambini grand**i**
the big boy	*the big boys*
il padre grand**e**	i padri grand**i**
the big father	*the big fathers*
Feminine	
la bambina alt**a**	le bambine alt**e**
the tall girl	*the tall girls*
la madre alt**a**	le madri alt**e**
the tall mother	*the tall mothers*
la bambina grand**e**	le bambine grand**i**
the big girl	*the big girls*
la madre grand**e**	le madri grand**i**
the big mother	*the big mothers*

Dialogo

Here's another dialogue showing you how someone might ask for directions:

SIGNORA: Scusi, sa dov'è un bancomat?	*Excuse me, do you know where there's an automatic teller?*
VIGILE: In via Boccaccio.	*On Boccaccio Street.*
SIGNORA: Come si fa per andarci?	*How does one get there?*
VIGILE: Vada a sud per un po'.	*Go south for a bit.*
SIGNORA: È vicino alla chiesa?	*Is it near the church?*
VIGILE: Sì. È proprio davanti. Non può sbagliare!	*Yes. Right in front of it. You can't go wrong!*

NEW VOCABULARY

andarci (andare + ci)	to go there	**potere**	to be able to, can
bancomat (*m.*)	automatic teller	**proprio**	just, right
chiesa	church	**un po'**	a bit
davanti	in front	**vigile** (véeh-jeeh-leh) (*m.*)	traffic policeman
fare	to do, to make		

Memory practice

Fill in the blanks with the appropriate words and expressions. Do this from memory, and then go back and check your answers.

Scusi, sa dov'è un _____?

In _____ Boccaccio.

Come si fa per _____?

Vada a _____ per un po'.

È vicino alla _____?

Sì. È proprio _____. Non può sbagliare!

Language notes

In this dialogue, you have come across yet another two important irregular verbs, **fare** and **potere**. In the present indicative they are conjugated as follows:

fare (to do, to make)

(io) faccio	*I do, I am doing*
(tu) fai	*you do, you are doing* (fam.)
(Lei) fa	*you do, you are doing* (pol.)
(lui) fa	*he does, he is doing*
(lei) fa	*she does, she is doing*
(noi) facciamo	*we do, we are doing*
(voi) fate	*you do, you are doing* (pl.)
(loro) fanno	*they do, they are doing*

potere (to be able to, to can)

(io) posso	*I can, I am able to*
(tu) puoi	*you can, you are able to* (fam.)
(Lei) può	*you can, you are able to* (pol.)
(lui) può	*he can, he is able to*
(lei) può	*she can, she is able to*
(noi) possiamo	*we can, we are able to*
(voi) potete	*you can, you are able to* (pl.)
(loro) possono (póhs-soh-noh)	*they can, they are able to*

Note that **si** is the generic person *one*. So, **si fa** means *one does*. When asking for directions, you'll need to know the following:

nord	*north*
sud	*south*
est	*east*
ovest	*west*

Indicate the correct form of the verbs **dovere**, **andare**, **dire**, **fare**, and **potere**.

EXAMPLE: io _devo_   _vado_   _dico_   _faccio_   _posso_

1. tu   _____ _____ _____ _____ _____
2. lui   _____ _____ _____ _____ _____
3. noi   _____ _____ _____ _____ _____
4. voi   _____ _____ _____ _____ _____
5. loro _____ _____ _____ _____ _____
6. io   _____ _____ _____ _____ _____

Put the appropriate form of the indefinite article before the following nouns.

7. _____ semaforo

8. _____ strada

9. _____ studente

10. _____ studentessa

11. _____ zio

12. _____ zia

Give the corresponding singular or plural form of each phrase as the case may be.

SINGULAR	PLURAL
13. il bambino bello	_____
14. _____	le donne belle
15. il vigile alto	_____
16. _____	le madri alte
17. la casa grande	_____
18. _____	i bambini grandi

Carry out the following conversation tasks.

19. Ask someone if they can tell you where Dante Street is.

   _____

20. Tell someone to go right for a block and then to turn left at the traffic lights.

   _____

21. Ask if you have to cross the road.

   _____

22. Tell someone to go straight ahead for three more blocks.

   _____

23. Ask if Macchiavelli Street is there.

_____

24. Point out an automatic teller to someone (_Remember_ **ecco**?)

_____

25. Ask "How does one get there?"

_____

26. Tell someone to go north for a bit.

_____

27. Tell someone that it is near the church.

_____

28. Tell someone that it is right in front of the church.

_____

29. Tell someone that he/she cannot go wrong.

_____

30. Tell someone to go south and then east for a bit.

_____

On the phone and mobile devices

Dialogo

Here's how a phone conversation might sound in Italian:

LAURA:	Pronto! Chi parla?	_Hello! Who's speaking?_
VINCENZO:	Laura, sono Vincenzo.	_Laura, it's Vincenzo._
LAURA:	Ciao, Vincenzo. Che vuoi?	_Hi, Vincenzo. What do you want?_
VINCENZO:	C'è tuo fratello?	_Is your brother there?_
LAURA:	No, non c'è.	_No, he's not here._
VINCENZO:	Non importa. Telefono più tardi.	_It doesn't matter. I'll phone later._
LAURA:	Arrivederci.	_Good-bye._

NEW VOCABULARY

non importa	it doesn't matter	**Pronto!**	Hello!
parlare	to speak	**telefonare**	to phone
più	more	**volere**	to want

Memory practice

Fill in the blanks with the appropriate words and expressions. Do this from memory, and then go back and check your answers.

Pronto! Chi _____?
Laura, _____ Vincenzo.
Ciao, Vincenzo. Che _____?
C'è tuo _____?
No, non _____.
Non importa. _____ più tardi.
Arrivederci.

Language notes

Note that to say who you are on the phone you say **sono...** (*I am*), not *it is*, as in English.

In the previous dialogue you have come across another useful irregular verb: **volere**. Here's its conjugation in the present indicative:

volere (*to want*)	
(io) voglio	*I want*
(tu) vuoi	*you want* (fam.)
(Lei) vuole	*you want* (pol.)
(lui) vuole	*he wants*
(lei) vuole	*she wants*
(noi) vogliamo	*we want*
(voi) volete	*you want* (pl.)
(loro) vogliono (vóh-lyoh-noh)	*they want*

Dialogo

Here is an example of what you might say if you wanted to send a text message:

MARCO: Maria, ti chiamo col mio cellulare stasera. Va bene? — *Maria, I'll call you on my cell tonight, OK?*

MARIA: È meglio mandarmi un SMS. — *It's better to send me a text.*

MARCO: Non ho il mio dispositivo mobile. — *I don't have my mobile device.*

MARIA: Allora, manda un messaggino col cellulare, va bene? — *Then send me a text with your cell, OK?*

MARCO: D'accordo. — *Fine (I agree).*

NEW VOCABULARY

cellulare	cell phone	**mandarmi (= mandare + mi)**	to send me
chiamare	to call	**meglio**	better
d'accordo	fine, I agree	**messaggino**	text, message
dispositivo	device	**mobile (móh-beeh-leh)**	mobile
mandare	to send	**SMS**	text message

Memory practice

Fill in the blanks with the appropriate words and expressions. Do this from memory, and then go back and check your answers.

Maria, ti _____ col mio cellulare stasera. Va bene?
È _____ mandarmi un SMS.
Non ho il mio dispositivo _____.
Allora, manda un messaggino col _____, va bene?
D'accordo.

Language notes

Note that **manda** is yet another imperative form.
   It is now time to summarize the forms of the definite article:

* **lo** before a masculine noun (or adjective) beginning with **z** or **s** + consonant: **lo zio** (*the uncle*), **lo studente** (*the student*)
* **il** before all other masculine nouns (or adjectives) beginning with any other consonant: **il bambino** (*the little boy*), **il vigile** (*the traffic policeman*).
* **la** before feminine nouns beginning with any consonant: **la zia** (*the aunt*), **la studentessa** (*the female student*)
* **l'** before masculine and feminine nouns beginning with any vowel: **l'americano** (*the American man*), **l'americana** (*the American woman*)

The corresponding plural forms are as follows.

SINGULAR	PLURAL
lo	**gli**
lo zio	gli zii
il	**i**
il vigile	i vigili
la	**le**
la casa	le case
l' (*m.*)	**gli**
l'americano	gli americani
l' (*f.*)	**le**
l'americana	le americane

EXERCISE
3·3

Give the corresponding singular or plural form of each phrase as the case may be.

SINGULAR	PLURAL
1. il bambino	_____
2. _____	le strade
3. lo studente	_____
4. _____	le avventure
5. l'anno	_____

6. _____   gli euro

7. il caffè   _____

8. _____   gli uomini

*Indicate the appropriate form of **volere** according to the given person.*

9. (io) _____

10. (loro) _____

11. (tu) _____

12. (lui/lei) _____

13. (noi) _____

14. (voi) _____

Carry out the following conversation tasks.

15. Tell Giovanni that you will call him tonight on your cell.

_____

16. Say that it's better to send you a text message.

_____

17. Say that you do not have a mobile device.

_____

18. Say hello on the phone.

_____

19. Ask who's speaking.

_____

20. Say that it is you (speaking).

_____

21. Ask Laura what she wants.

_____

22. Now ask Mrs. Verdi, politely of course, what she wants.

_____

23. Say that he's not in.

_____

24. Say that it doesn't matter.

_____

25. Say that you'll call later.

_____

People

Knowing how to describe people, flirt a bit, portray character, and talk about family relationships adds up to an important conversation skill. This chapter will show you how to hone that skill in Italian.

Describing and flirting

Dialogo

Here's how one might describe an attractive person:

SARA: Natalia, guarda che uomo bello!	*Natalia, look at the handsome man!*
NATALIA: Troppo alto per me! E poi, non mi piacciono gli uomini biondi!	*Too tall for me! And then, I don't like blond men.*
SARA: Non il biondo! Il bruno, con gli occhi blu.	*Not the blond one. The dark-haired one with blue eyes.*
NATALIA: Non sembra intelligente!	*He doesn't seem intelligent!*
SARA: Sei troppo fastidiosa! Sembra molto simpatico!	*You're too fussy! I bet that he's very charming!*
NATALIA: Allora, che cosa aspetti?	*Then what are you waiting for?*
SARA: Ci provo.	*I'm going to try.*

NEW VOCABULARY

aspettare	to wait for	**intelligente**	intelligent
biondo	blond	**occhio (óhk-kyoh)**	eye
blu	dark blue	**provarci**	to go ahead
bruno	dark-haired	(= **provare** + **ci**)	and try
fastidioso	fussy	**provare**	to try
guardare	to look at, to watch	**simpatico**	nice, charming

Memory practice

Fill in the blanks with the appropriate words and expressions. Do this from memory, and then go back and check your answers.

Natalia, _____ che uomo bello!

Troppo alto per me! E poi, non mi piacciono gli uomini _____!

Non il biondo! Il bruno, con gli _____ blu.

Non sembra _____!

Sei troppo _____! Sembra molto simpatico!

Allora, che cosa _____?

Ci provo.

Language notes

In this dialogue you have come across a number of new adjectives, which are useful for describing people. They are treated just like the other ones you learned about, except **blu**, which is invariable: **l'occhio blu** (*the blue eye*), **gli occhi blu** (*the blue eyes*).

Descriptive adjectives are best learned in contrasting pairs. Here are a few:

TRAIT	OPPOSITE
alto (*tall*)	basso (*short*)
bello (*nice, beautiful*)	brutto (*ugly*)
grande (*big*)	piccolo (péehk-koh-loh) (*little, small*)
intelligente (*intelligent*)	stupido (stóoh-peeh-doh) (*stupid*)
timido (*timid, shy*)	sicuro (*secure, sure*)

It is now time to summarize prepositional contractions. The prepositions that always contract before the definite article are: **a** (*to, at*), **di** (*of*), **da** (*from*), **in** (*in*), and **su** (*on*). The following chart summarizes the contractions:

+	IL	I	LO	L'	GLI	LA	LE
a	al	ai	allo	all'	agli	alla	alle
da	dal	dai	dallo	dall'	dagli	dalla	dalle
di	del	dei	dello	dell'	degli	della	delle
in	nel	nei	nello	nell'	negli	nella	nelle
su	sul	sui	sullo	sull'	sugli	sulla	sulle

Contraction does not apply to the other prepositions, except for **con** for which they are optional. In practice only the form **col** = **con** + **il** is used commonly.

Dialogo

Here is an analogous conversation to the previous one.

MARCELLO: Giovanni, guarda quella donna bella!	*Giovanni, look at that beautiful woman!*
GIOVANNI: Sì. È proprio bella!	*Yes. She's really beautiful!*
MARCELLO: È senz'altro sposata!	*She's likely married!*
GIOVANNI: Forse no, perché non porta l'anello.	*Maybe not, because she's not wearing a ring.*

MARCELLO: È vero. Ma sono un po' timido per presentarmi.

It's true. But I'm a little shy to introduce myself.

GIOVANNI: Non ci credo. Sei sempre così sicuro di te.

I don't believe it. You're always so sure of yourself.

MARCELLO: Va bene. Ci provo.

OK. I'll try.

NEW VOCABULARY			
anello	finger ring	**presentarmi**	to introduce myself
così	so	(**= presentare + mi**)	
crederci	to believe it	**proprio**	really
(**= credere + ci**)		**senz'altro**	without doubt, likely
credere	to believe	**senza**	without
forse	maybe	**sicuro**	sure
portare	to wear	**timido** (téeh-meeh-doh)	timid, shy
presentare	to present, to introduce		

Memory practice

Fill in the blanks with the appropriate words and expressions. Do this from memory, and then go back and check your answers.

Giovanni, guarda _____ donna bella!

Sì. È _____ bella!

È, _____, sposata!

Forse no, perché non _____ l'anello.

È vero. Ma sono un po' _____ per presentarmi.

Non ci _____. Sei sempre così sicuro di te.

Va bene. Ci _____.

Language notes

The word **quella** is part of the demonstrative system of Italian. The system has two parts. First, there is the demonstrative indicating relative nearness: the forms of **questo** (*this, these*). Here are its forms. Note that like the article it precedes the noun, agreeing with it in gender and number.

SINGULAR	PLURAL
Masculine	
quest**o** cornetto	quest**i** cornetti
this croissant	*these croissants*
Feminine	
quest**a** commessa	quest**e** commesse
this female clerk	*these female clerks*

The second part of the demonstrative system is that indicating distance: the forms of **quello** (*that, those*). It takes the following forms. Note that they vary in the same way that the definite article does.

SINGULAR	PLURAL
Masculine	
[Before **z** or **s** + **consonant**]	
quello	quegli
quello studente	quegli studenti
that student	*those students*
[Before any other consonant]	
quel	quei
quel bambino	quei bambini
that boy	*those boys*
[Before any vowel]	
quell'	quegli
quell'americano	quegli americani
that American	*those Americans*
Feminine	
[Before any consonant]	
quella	quelle
quella commessa	quelle commesse
that female clerk	*those female clerks*
[Before any vowel]	
quell'	quelle
quell'italiana	quelle italiane
that female Italian	*those female Italians*

EXERCISE
4·1

Give the opposite phrase.

EXAMPLE: quel bambino grande   *quel bambino piccolo*

1. questo uomo timido _____

2. quello studente intelligente _____

3. questi commessi alti _____

4. quegli uomini brutti _____

5. questo signore intelligente _____

6. quell'americano piccolo _____

7. quegli italiani alti _____

8. questa donna bella _____

9. queste bambine sicure _____

10. quella casa grande _____

11. quelle case belle _____

12. quell'americana alta _____

13. quelle americane basse _____

Now complete each phrase with the appropriate form of the prepositional contraction.

EXAMPLE: *in the* strada   *nella strada*

14. *at the* semaforo _____

15. *from the* commessi _____

16. *of the* zio _____

17. *in the* occhio _____

18. *on the* SMS (*Be careful!*) _____

19. *to the* donne _____

20. *in the* strada _____

21. *of the* bambini _____

22. *of the* uomini _____

Carry out the following conversation tasks.

23. First, tell your lady friend to look at the handsome man.

_____

24. Now tell your male friend to look at the beautiful woman.

_____

25. Say that the man is too tall for you.

_____

26. Say that you like blond men with blue eyes.

_____

27. Say that you do not like dark-haired men who are too tall.

_____

28. Say that he doesn't seem intelligent, but he seems very charming.

_____

29. Tell your friend that she is too fussy.

_____

30. Ask your friend, then, what she's waiting for.

_____

31. Say OK that you'll give it a try.

_____

32. Say that this woman here is really beautiful.

_____

33. Say that that woman is likely to be married, because she is wearing a ring.

_____

34. Say that maybe the woman is a little shy.

_____

35. Say that you don't believe it, because she is always sure of herself (**di sé**).

_____

Character

Dialogo

The following dialogue is also about a potential amorous encounter. More importantly, it shows how character can be talked about; and from it you will learn a few more ways to describe people.

BRUNA: Mio fratello è molto noioso!	_My brother is really annoying!_
MARISA: No, io lo trovo molto simpatico e vivace.	_No, I find him (to be) very nice and vivacious._
BRUNA: Non lo conosci come me!	_You don't know him like I do!_
MARISA: A me, sembra un ragazzo sincero, educato e anche assai carino!	_To me, he seems like a sincere, well-mannered guy and also quite cute!_
BRUNA: Capisco. Ti sei innamorata, vero?	_I get it (I understand). You've fallen in love, haven't you?_
MARISA: Sì, un po'!	_Yes, a bit!_

NEW VOCABULARY			
assai	quite	**noioso**	annoying
capire	to understand	**ragazzo**	boy, youth
carino	cute	**sincero**	sincere
come	like	**trovare**	to find
educato	well-mannered	**vivace**	lively, vivacious
essere innamorato	to be/fall in love		

Memory practice

Fill in the blanks with the appropriate words and expressions. Do this from memory, and then go back and check your answers.

Mio fratello è molto _____!

No, io lo trovo molto simpatico e _____.

Non lo _____ come me!

A me, sembra un _____ sincero, educato e anche assai _____!

_____. Ti sei _____, vero?

Sì, un po'!

Language notes

In this chapter you have come across a third-conjugation verb: **capire** (*to understand*). Recall that first-conjugation verbs end in **-are**, second in **-ere**. There are no others to learn about, especially in a brief introduction to the language. There are two types of third-conjugation verbs. Verbs such as **capire** and **finire** belong to the first type in which an **-isc** is added to all the persons except the first (**noi**) and second (**voi**) plural. The other type does not have this. A typical verb for this second type is **dormire** (*to sleep*). Compare their present indicative conjugations:

capire (*to understand*)		**dormire** (*to sleep*)	
(io) capisco	*I understand*	(io) dormo	*I sleep, I am sleeping*
(tu) capisci	*you understand (fam.)*	(tu) dormi	*you sleep, you are sleeping (fam.)*
(Lei) capisce	*you understand (pol.)*	(Lei) dorme	*you sleep, you are sleeping (pol.)*
(lui) capisce	*he understands*	(lui) dorme	*he sleeps, he is sleeping*
(lei) capisce	*she understands*	(lei) dorme	*she sleeps, she is sleeping*
(noi) capiamo	*we understand*	(noi) dormiamo	*we sleep, we are sleeping*
(voi) capite	*you understand (pl.)*	(voi) dormite	*you sleep, you are sleeping (pl.)*
(loro) capiscono	*they understand*	(loro) dormono	*they sleep, they are sleeping*

You will have to simply consult a dictionary or glossary to find out which verb is conjugated in which way.

Also note that **ragazzo**, as we saw in the previous dialogue, means a boy or adolescent, and the corresponding feminine form is **ragazza**.

Incidentally, you have been using **di** as a genitive preposition throughout. It generally translates as the *'s* of English possession. Note that it may have to be contracted.

il fratello **di** Maria	*Maria's brother* (literally: *the brother of Maria*)
la zia **della** donna	*the woman's aunt*

Dialogo

This dialogue is very similar to the previous one. It's all about character portrayal and falling in love.

ALESSANDRO: Mi piace molto la tua amica!	*I like you're friend a lot!*
BRUNA: Chi? Marisa?	*Who? Marisa?*
ALESSANDRO: Sì, proprio lei. È una ragazza molto amichevole e sincera.	*Yes, precisely her. She's a very friendly and sincere girl.*
BRUNA: Sei innamorato?	*Are you in love?*

ALESSANDRO: No, mi piacciono le ragazze ottimiste e felici.

No, I like optimistic and happy girls.

BRUNA: Capisco. Siete tutti e due innamorati.

I get it. You're both in love.

NEW VOCABULARY

amichevole (ah-meeh-kéh-voh-leh)	friendly	**ottimista**	optimistic
amico (-a)	friend	**tutti e due**	both
felice	happy		

Memory practice

Fill in the blanks with the appropriate words and expressions. Do this from memory, and then go back and check your answers.

Mi piace molto la tua _____!

Chi? Marisa?

Sì, proprio lei. È una _____ molto amichevole e sincera.

Sei _____?

No, mi piacciono le ragazze ottimiste e _____.

Capisco. Siete _____ e due innamorati.

Language notes

Note that the plural of **amico** (*male friend*) is **amici** (ah-méeh-cheeh), with the soft sound of **c**; whereas for **amica** (*female friend*), it is **amiche** (ah-méeh-keh), with the hard sound of **c**.

The word **ottimista** is both masculine and feminine, as is **barista** (which you came across previously). The plural forms of each, however, change according to gender, namely to **-i** (*masculine*) and **-e** (*feminine*). This applies to all forms ending in **-ista**. There are not many of these.

SINGULAR	PLURAL
Masculine	
l'ottimista	gli ottimist**i**
il barista	i barist**i**
Feminine	
l'ottimista	le ottimist**e**
la barista	le barist**e**

Throughout this and previous chapters you have come across snippets of the possessive: *my*, *your*, and so on. The time has come to summarize its forms. Note that the definite article is part of the possessive and that the possessive is an adjective agreeing in number and gender with the noun.

	MASCULINE		FEMININE	
	SINGULAR	PLURAL	SINGULAR	PLURAL
my	il mio (amico)	i miei (amici)	la mia (amica)	le mie (amiche)
your (fam.)	il tuo (cornetto)	i tuoi (cornetti)	la tua (casa)	le tue (case)

continued

	MASCULINE		FEMININE	
	SINGULAR	PLURAL	SINGULAR	PLURAL
your (pol.)	il Suo (cornetto)	i Suoi (cornetti)	la Sua (casa)	le Sue (case)
his/her	il suo (amico)	i suoi (amici)	la sua (amica)	le sue (amiche)
our	il nostro (libro)	i nostri (libri)	la nostra (casa)	le nostre (case)
your (pl.)	il vostro (amico)	i vostri (amici)	la vostra (amica)	le vostre (amiche)
their	il loro (professore)	i loro (professori)	la loro (dottoressa)	le loro (dottoresse)

Note that the **loro** form is invariable. Also, when used with a family member or a relative in the singular, the article is dropped. If the noun is plural or modified (by an adjective) the article is restored.

mio padre	*my father*
nostro zio	*our uncle*
sua madre	*his/her mother*
tua zia	*your aunt*

But:

il mio padre alto	*my tall father*
i nostri zii	*our uncles*
la sua madre bella	*his/her beautiful mother*
le tue zie	*your aunts*

The exception is, again, **loro**, which must be used with the article: **il loro padre**. This is changing, however, so that it also can be used without nowadays: **loro padre**.

Finally, note that the **suo** forms translate as either *his* or *her*, according to context. Thus, **suo fratello** can be either *his brother* or *her brother*, as you can see below:

Marco è il fratello di Maria?	*Is Marco Maria's brother?*
Sì, è suo fratello.	*Yes, he is her brother.*
Marco è il fratello di Giovanni?	*Is Marco Giovanni's brother?*
Sì, è suo fratello.	*Yes, he is his brother.*

EXERCISE
4·2

Translate the following sentences into Italian.

1. He understands a lot.

_____

2. We finish at five o'clock, and then we will be going to Maria's house.

_____

3. Maria's brother sleeps till (**fino a**) noon.

_____

Put the appropriate ending on each verb.

4. Loro non cap _____.

5. Le amiche di Maria dorm _____ sempre fino a tardi.

6. Quei ragazzi non fin _____ fino alle sette.

7. Tu non cap _____, vero?

Give the appropriate possessive as indicated, and then turn the whole phrase into the plural. Follow the example.

EXAMPLE: *my* amica   *la mia amica*   *le mie amiche*

8. *my* amico   _____   _____

9. *your* (*fam.*) zia   _____   _____

10. *your* (*fam.*) zio   _____   _____

11. *his* amica   _____   _____

12. *her* amica   _____   _____

13. *our* padre   _____   _____

14. *our* professore   _____   _____

15. *your* (*pl.*) fratello   _____   _____

16. *your* (*pol.*) casa   _____   _____

17. *their* aunt   _____   _____

18. *their* amico   _____   _____

Carry out the following conversation tasks.

19. Say that your brother is annoying, but that he is quite cute.

_____

20. Say that you find your female friend charming and vivacious.

_____

21. Say that you do not know your brother's male friend.

_____

22. Say that your female friend's brother seems to be a sincere and well-mannered youth.

_____

23. Say that you get it!

_____

24. Ask a female friend if she is in love.

_____

25. Now ask a male friend if he is in love.

_____

26. Now ask your friends if they are in love.

_____

27. Say that you like happy and optimistic guys. (use **ragazzo**)

_____

28. Say that you also like happy and optimistic girls. (use **ragazza**)

_____

_____

Family relationships

Dialogo

Here is the type of brief conversation that may take place in a typical household:

SORELLA:	Alessandro, mi presti dei soldi?	_Alessandro, can you lend me some money?_
FRATELLO:	No, non posso!	_No, I can't!_
SORELLA:	Sei proprio come la mamma!	_You're just like Mom!_
FRATELLO:	E tu come il papà!	_And you're like Dad!_
SORELLA:	Perché non chiedi al nonno o alla nonna?	_Why don't you ask Granddad or Grandma?_
FRATELLO:	Hai ragione! Loro sono generosi!	_You're right! They're generous!_

NEW VOCABULARY

avere ragione	to be right	**prestare**	to lend
chiedere (kyéh-deh-reh)	to ask for	**soldi**	money
generoso	generous		

Memory practice

Fill in the blanks with the appropriate words and expressions. Do this from memory, and then go back and check your answers.

Alessandro, mi _____ dei soldi?

No, non _____!

Sei proprio come la _____!

E tu come il _____!

Perché non _____ al nonno o alla nonna?

Hai _____! Loro sono generosi!

Language notes

Note that **avere ragione** is like **avere fame**. It means, literally, _to have reason_: **ho ragione** (_I am right_), **lui ha ragione** (_he is right_).

Note that to say *some*, just use the prepositional contraction **di** + definite article.

del caffè	*some coffee*
dei soldi	*some money*
degli amici	*some friends*
delle case	*some houses*
delle donne	*some women*

Here is a list of the words for common family members, some of which you have already come across:

MALE	FEMALE
nonno (*grandfather*)	nonna (*grandmother*)
padre (*father*)	madre (*mother*)
fratello (*brother*)	sorella (*sister*)
mamma (*mom*)	papà (*dad*)
zio (*uncle*)	zia (*aunt*)
cugino (*cousin*)	cugina (*cousin*)
figlio (*son*)	figlia (*daughter*)
marito (*husband*)	moglie (*wife*)

Note that some adjectives, like **piccolo** or **grande**, can come before or after the noun: **il piccolo bambino/il bambino piccolo, la casa nuova/la nuova casa**. This also applies to **bello**, but there are changes in this case to the form, which will be discussed later.

Dialogo

Here is some more in-family chatter:

SARA: Alessandro, che pensi della nostra piccola cugina che è nata ieri?	*Alessandro, what do you think of our little cousin who was born yesterday?*
ALESSANDRO: Lei assomiglia a suo padre, nostro zio.	*She looks like her father, our uncle.*
SARA: E anche un po' a sua madre, nostra zia.	*And also a bit like her mother, our aunt.*
ALESSANDRO: Sì, hai ragione. È molto carina.	*Yes, you're right. She's very cute.*
SARA: Come tutta la nostra famiglia.	*Like our whole family.*

NEW VOCABULARY

assomigliare a	to look like	**ieri**	yesterday
famiglia	family	**pensare**	to think

Memory practice

Fill in the blanks with the appropriate words and expressions. Do this from memory, and then go back and check your answers.

Alessandro, che _____ della nostra piccola cugina
che è _____ ieri?
Lei _____ a suo padre, nostro zio.

E anche un po' a _____ madre, nostra zia.

Sì, hai _____. È molto carina.

Come tutta la nostra _____.

Language notes

Note that **tutto** is an adjective in **tutta la famiglia** (*all the family*), **tutte le case** (*all the houses*), and so on. Recall that it is also part of the formula for *both*: **tutti e due**. In this case the ending reflects the gender.

tutt**i** e due i ragazzi   *both the boys*

tutt**e** e due le ragazze   *both the girls*

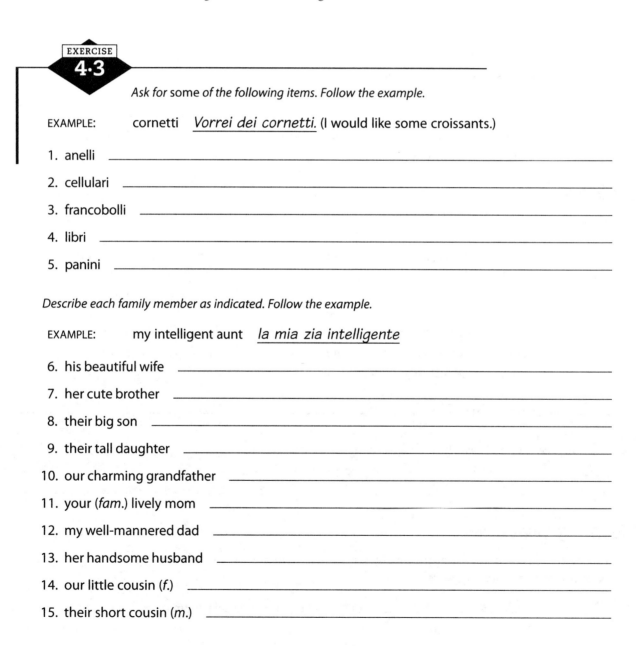

EXERCISE
4·3

Ask for some of the following items. Follow the example.

EXAMPLE: cornetti   *Vorrei dei cornetti.* (I would like some croissants.)

1. anelli _____

2. cellulari _____

3. francobolli _____

4. libri _____

5. panini _____

Describe each family member as indicated. Follow the example.

EXAMPLE: my intelligent aunt   *la mia zia intelligente*

6. his beautiful wife _____

7. her cute brother _____

8. their big son _____

9. their tall daughter _____

10. our charming grandfather _____

11. your (*fam.*) lively mom _____

12. my well-mannered dad _____

13. her handsome husband _____

14. our little cousin (*f.*) _____

15. their short cousin (*m.*) _____

Carry out the following conversation tasks.

16. Ask your brother, Alessandro, to lend you some money.

_____

17. Say that you cannot.

_____

18. Tell your brother that he is just like his dad.

_____

19. Tell your sister that she is just like her mom.

_____

20. Ask your brother why he doesn't ask Granddad or Grandma.

_____

21. Tell your sister that she's right and that she's also very generous.

_____

22. Ask your brother if your little female cousin was born yesterday.

_____

23. Say that she looks like her mother.

_____

24. Say that your whole family is nice.

_____

Jobs and homes

Knowing how to speak about jobs, what to say at a job interview, and how to talk about homes is an obvious conversational skill to be acquired. This chapter will show you how to do so.

Jobs

Dialogo

Choosing a career is the theme of the following brief conversation. Take special note of the words for various professions.

MARCO: Maria, conosci un bravo dentista?	*Maria, do you know a good dentist?*
MARIA: Perché? Hai mal di denti?	*Why? Do you have a toothache?*
MARCO: No, voglio diventare dentista o medico e allora voglio qualche consiglio.	*No, I want to be a dentist or a doctor, and thus I want some advice.*
MARIA: Dentista, tu? Impossibile! Forse avvocato o anche architetto, ma non ti vedo come dentista.	*You, a dentist? Maybe a lawyer or even an architect, but I don't see you as a dentist.*
MARCO: Forse hai ragione.	*Maybe you're right.*

NEW VOCABULARY

architetto	architect	**diventare**	to become
avvocato	lawyer	**impossibile**	impossible
bravo	good (*at something*)	**mal di denti**	toothache
consiglio	advice	**medico** (méh-deeh-koh)	medical doctor
dentista (*m./f.*)	dentist	**o**	or

Memory practice

Fill in the blanks with the appropriate words and expressions. Do this from memory, and then go back and check your answers.

Maria, conosci un _____ dentista?

Perché? Hai mal di _____?

No, voglio diventare dentista o _____ e allora voglio _____
consiglio.

Dentista, tu? Impossibile! Forse _____ o anche architetto, ma non ti
_____ come dentista.

Forse hai _____.

Language notes

As mentioned previously, some adjectives can be placed before a noun. When they are, two things can happen, either separately or in tandem: (1) there is a meaning change, and/or (2) they change in form. An example of (1) is **grande**. When it is placed after a noun it means *big*, and when in front it can also mean *great*:

un libro grande	*a big book* (*in size*)
un grande libro	*a great book*

The adjectives **buono** (*good*) and **bello** (*beautiful*) are examples of (2). Appearing after a noun, they are regular adjectives ending in **-o**. But before nouns, they change as follows:

Buono has analogous forms to the indefinite article. In addition, it has plural forms. Notice that the article in front of **buono** has to be adapted as well to agree with it. So, for example, the **uno** in **uno zio** is changed to **un** because it is now in front of the **b** of **buono**.

- ◆ **buono** before a masculine noun (or adjective) beginning with **z** or **s** + consonant: **un buono zio** (*a good uncle*), **un buono studente** (*a good student*). The plural form is **buoni**: **i buoni zii** (*the good uncles*), **i buoni studenti** (*the good students*).
- ◆ **buon** before all other masculine nouns (or adjectives): **un buon bambino** (*a good child*), **un buon uomo** (*a good man*). Again the plural is **buoni**: **i buoni bambini** (*the good children*), **i buoni uomini** (*the good men*).
- ◆ **buona** before feminine nouns beginning with any consonant: **una buona zia** (*a good aunt aunt*), **una buona studentessa** (*a good female student*). The plural form is **buone**: **le buone zie** (*the good aunts*), **le buone studentesse** (*the good students*).
- ◆ **buon'** before feminine nouns beginning with any vowel: **una buon'americana** (*a good American woman*), **una buon'avventura** (*a good adventure*). Again, the plural form is **buone**: **le buone americane** (*the good American women*), **le buone avventure** (*the good adventures*).

The forms of **bello** change in an analogous fashion to the definite article and the demonstrative **quello**.

SINGULAR	PLURAL
Masculine	
[Before **z** or **s** + **consonant**]	
bello	begli
il bello studente	i begli studenti
the handsome student	*the handsome students*
[Before any other consonant]	
bel	bei

continued

SINGULAR	PLURAL
il bel bambino	i bei bambini
the beautiful child	*the beautiful children*
[Before any vowel]	
bell'	begli
il bell'amico	i begli amici
the handsome friend	*the handsome friends*
Feminine	
[Before any consonant]	
bella	belle
la bella donna	le belle donne
the beautiful woman	*the beautiful women*
[Before any vowel]	
bell'	belle
la bell'italiana	le belle italiane
the beautiful Italian woman	*the beautiful Italian women*

Note that **qualche** means *some*, and it is followed by a singular noun even if it is a plural concept. It is an alternative to the **di + article** contraction you learned about in the previous chapter.

dei consigli = qualche consiglio	*some advice*
dei bambini = qualche bambino	*some children*
degli amici = qualche amico	*some friends*
delle case = qualche casa	*some houses*

Dialogo

The previous conversation continues. Take particular notice of the words for the professions and jobs mentioned.

MARCO: Maria, pensi che è forse meglio fare qualcosa di più pratico, come elettricista o barbiere?

Maria, do you think it is perhaps better to do something more practical, like an electrician or a barber?

MARIA: Sei impossibile, Marco! Secondo me, tu sei nato per essere insegnante.

You're impossible, Marco! In my opinion, you're a born teacher.

MARCO: No, non mi piace la scuola. Preferisco fare l'impiegato o anche un meccanico, piuttosto che insegnante.

No, I don't like school. I prefer to be an office worker or even a mechanic, rather than a teacher.

MARIA: Fa' quello che vuoi!

Do, whatever you want!

NEW VOCABULARY

barbiere (*m.*)	barber	**pratico (práh-teeh-koh)**	practical
elettricista (*m./f.*)	electrician	**preferire (isc)**	to prefer
impiegato (-a)	office worker	**qualcosa**	something
insegnante (*m./f.*)	teacher	**quello che**	that which, whatever

meccanico (meh-káh-neeh-koh)	mechanic	**scuola**	school
		secondo	according to
piuttosto	rather		

Memory practice

Fill in the blanks with the appropriate words and expressions. Do this from memory, and then go back and check your answers.

Maria, pensi che è forse meglio fare _____ di più pratico, come elettricista o _____?

Sei impossibile, Marco! _____ me, tu sei nato per essere insegnante.

No, non mi piace la _____. Preferisco fare _____ o anche un meccanico, piuttosto che _____.

Fa' _____ che vuoi!

Language notes

The form **Fa'** is an imperative. You have already come across imperative forms in previous chapters. To form the imperative of first-conjugation verbs, drop the -**are** and add the following endings:

girare (*to turn*)	
(tu) gir**a**	*turn (fam.)*
(Lei) gir**i**	*turn (pol.)*
(noi) gir**iamo**	*let's turn*
(voi) gir**ate**	*turn (pl.)*
(loro) gir**ino** (jéeh-reeh-noh)	*turn (pol. pl.)*

Note that there is a polite plural form (**Loro**). More will be said about it in due course. For now, just note that it is the plural of **Lei** forms, for example:

Signor Marchi, giri a destra!	*Mr. Marchi, turn right!*
Signori, girino a destra!	*Gentlemen, turn right!*

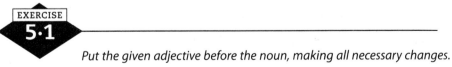

EXERCISE
5·1

Put the given adjective before the noun, making all necessary changes.

EXAMPLE: uno studente buono   *un buono studente*

1. gli zii buoni _____

2. le ragazze belle _____

3. la signora bella _____

4. l'amica bella _____

5. gli amici belli _____

6. l'uomo bello _____

7. l'uomo buono _____

8. lo zio bello _____

9. il panino buono _____

*Now give the equivalent for some. If you are given **dei panini**, the equivalent would be **qualche panino**; if instead, you are given **qualche amico**, give **degli amici**.*

10. delle amiche _____

11. qualche studente _____

12. dei cornetti _____

13. qualche libro _____

Tell the following people to do the indicated things.

14. Tell Marco to speak Italian.

_____

15. Tell Mr. Verdi to speak Italian.

_____

16. Tell Giovanni and Maria (together) to wait here.

_____

17. Tell a group of young ladies to wait here.

_____

Carry out the following conversation tasks.

18. Ask your sister if she knows a good lawyer or a good dentist.

_____

19. Ask your brother if he has a toothache.

_____

20. Say that you want to become a medical doctor or maybe an architect.

_____

21. Say that it's impossible.

_____

22. Ask your sister if it is perhaps better to do something more practical.

_____

23. Tell your brother that in your opinion, he is born to be a teacher.

_____

24. Say that you prefer to be a mechanic rather than an office worker.

_____

25. Tell your brother to do whatever he wants.

_____

Job interviews

Dialogo

The following dialogue exemplifies what someone looking for a job might say

BRUNA: Scusi, cerco lavoro nella Sua ditta.

Excuse me, I am looking for a job in your company.

SIGNORE: Ha mai lavorato in una ditta di informatica?

Have you ever worked for a computer (informatics) company?

BRUNA: No, ma ho una laurea in matematica. E ho creato diversi programmi all'università.

No, but I have a degree in mathematics. And I created several (computer) programs at the university.

SIGNORE: Ottimo. Ha qualche esperienza di lavoro?

Excellent. Do you have any work experience?

BRUNA: Sì, ho lavorato per una banca due anni fa.

Yes, I worked for a bank two years ago.

SIGNORE: Per il momento va bene così. Torni domani per un'intervista ufficiale, va bene?

For the time being this is all (it's OK like this). Come back tomorrow for an official interview, OK?

BRUNA: Certo. Grazie.

Of course. Thank you.

NEW VOCABULARY

banca	bank	**laurea**	degree
cercare	to search for, to look for	**lavorare**	to work
creare	to create	**lavoro**	work, job
ditta	company (*business*)	**mai**	ever, never
diverso	diverse, various, several	**matematica**	mathematics
esperienza	experience	**momento**	moment
fa	ago	**programma** (*m.*)	program
informatica	computer, informatics	**ufficiale**	official
intervista	interview	**università** (*f.*)	university

Memory practice

Fill in the blanks with the appropriate words and expressions. Do this from memory, and then go back and check your answers.

Scusi, _____ lavoro nella Sua ditta.

Ha mai _____ in una ditta di informatica?

No, ma ho una laurea in matematica. E ho _____ diversi
    programmi all'università.

Ottimo. Ha qualche esperienza di _____?

Sì, ho _____ per una banca due anni fa.

Per il momento va bene così. _____ domani per un'intervista
    ufficiale, va bene?

Certo. _____.

Language notes

The verb **cercare** retains the hard sound in its conjugations. So an **h** is added before an -**i** ending. In the present indicative, this is required for these two forms: **tu cerchi** and **noi cerchiamo**; in the imperative, it is required for these three forms: **(Lei) cerchi, (noi) cerchiamo, (Loro) cerchino**.

Note that you have come across your first past tense—the present perfect of first-conjugation verbs. It is made up of two parts: an auxiliary verb and a past participle. To form the past participle, drop the -**are** and add –**ato**.

parl**are** (*to speak*)	parl**ato** (*spoken*)
gir**are** (*to turn*)	gir**ato** (*turned*)

The auxiliary verb is either **avere** or **essere** in the present indicative (which you already know). For now, you have come across verbs using **avere**. Here is **lavorare** completely conjugated for you. You will learn more about this tense in subsequent chapters.

(io) ho lavorato	*I have worked, I worked*
(tu) hai lavorato	*you have worked, you worked* (fam.)
(Lei) ha lavorato	*you have worked, you worked* (pol.)
(lui) ha lavorato	*he has worked, he worked*
(lei) ha lavorato	*she has worked, she worked*
(noi) abbiamo lavorato	*we have worked, we worked*
(voi) avete lavorato	*you have worked, you worked* (pl.)
(loro) hanno lavorato	*they have worked, they worked*

Note that the plural of **banca** is **banche**, showing that the hard sound is retained. This applies to all nouns and adjectives ending in -**ca**.

Finally, **programma,** and any noun ending in -**amma**, is a masculine noun. Its plural form is **programmi**.

il nuovo programma	i nuovi programmi
the new program	*the new programs*

Dialogo

The following conversation is Bruna's interview:

BRUNA:	Eccomi di nuovo.	*Here I am again.*
SIGNORE:	Va bene. Le faccio una serie di domande. Quanti anni ha?	*OK. I am going to ask you a series of questions. How old are you?*
BRUNA:	Ho ventinove anni.	*I am twenty-nine.*
SIGNORE:	Qual è il Suo indirizzo?	*What's your address?*
BRUNA:	Abito in centro, in via Petrarca, numero trentasei.	*I live downtown at 36 Petrarch Street.*
SIGNORE:	Qual è il Suo stato civile?	*What's your marital status?*
BRUNA:	Sono single.	*I'm single.*
SIGNORE:	Va bene così. La chiamo la prossima settimana.	*OK for now. I'll call you next week.*

NEW VOCABULARY

centro	downtown, center of town		**quale**	which, what
di nuovo	again		**serie**	series
domanda	question		**settimana**	week
indirizzo	address		**stato civile**	marital status
numero (nóoh-meh-roh)	number			

Memory practice

Fill in the blanks with the appropriate words and expressions. Do this from memory, and then go back and check your answers.

_____ di nuovo.

Va bene. Le _____ una serie di _____. Quanti anni ha?

_____ ventinove anni.

Qual è il Suo _____?

Abito in _____, in via Petrarca, numero trentasei.

Qual è il Suo _____ civile?

_____ single.

Va bene così. La chiamo la _____ settimana.

Language notes

Let's continue with the imperative—this time of the second-conjugation verbs. Again, drop the infinitive ending of **-ere**, and add the following endings:

leggere (*to read*)	
(tu) legg**i** (léh-jeeh)	*read* (fam.)
(Lei) legg**a** (léh-gah)	*read* (pol.)
(noi) legg**iamo** (leh-jáh-moh)	*let's read*
(voi) legg**ete** (leh-jéh-teh)	*read* (pl.)
(loro) legg**ano** (léh-gah-noh)	*read* (pol. pl.)

Note that before **è** you simply drop the -e of **quale** without adding an apostrophe: **qual è**. With this dialogue, you have also come across a number of object pronouns (**mi, Le, La**), as you have in other chapters. These will be discussed in due course.

Put the given infinitives in the present perfect tense.

EXAMPLE: Io *parlare* al professore due giorni fa. *ho parlato*

1. Tu *aspettare* la mia amica, vero? _____

2. Lei, signora Verdi, *lavorare* già? _____

3. Mio fratello *mandare* un SMS a Bruna. _____

4. Noi *prestare* dei soldi al nonno. _____

5. Voi *sbagliare* tutto! _____

6. I miei amici *telefonare* due minuti fa. _____

Tell the following people to do the indicated things.

7. Tell Maria to read the beautiful novel.

_____

8. Tell Mrs. Verdi to ask for a coffee.

_____

9. Tell Marco and Maria (together) to take a little coffee.

_____

10. Tell a group of gentlemen to read the new book.

_____

Carry out the following conversation tasks.

11. Tell an employer that you are looking for a job in his/her company.

_____

12. Say that you have never worked in a computer (informatics) company.

_____

13. Say that you have a mathematics degree.

_____

14. Say that you have created several programs at the university.

_____

15. Say that you have some work experience.

16. Say that you worked for a bank several years ago.

17. Tell someone (politely) to come back next week for an official interview.

18. Say "Here I am again."

19. Ask someone (formally) how old he/she is.

20. Say that you want to ask a series of questions.

21. Ask someone (formally) what his/her address is.

22. Say that you live downtown.

23. Ask someone (formally) what his/her marital status is.

24. Say that you like those nice (beautiful) programs.

25. Ask your brother if he is looking for the bank.

Homes

Dialogo

Here's how a conversation between a husband and a wife who are house hunting might unfold:

MOGLIE: Questa casa è molto piccola.
This house is very small.

MARITO: Ma ha una bella cucina, due camere e un bagno grande.
But it has a nice kitchen, two bedrooms, and a big bathroom.

MOGLIE: Sì, e anche un salotto magnifico e una sala da pranzo eccezionale.
Yes, and also a magnificent living room and an exceptional dining room.

MARITO: Il garage, però, è un po' troppo piccolo.
The garage, however, is a bit too small.

MOGLIE: Ma ha un'entrata assai grande!
But it has a rather large entrance!

bagno	bathroom	**garage** (*m.*)	garage
camera (káh-meh-rah)	bedroom	**magnifico** (mah-nyéh-feeh-koh)	magnificent
cucina	kitchen	**però**	however
eccezionale	exceptional	**sala da pranzo**	dining room
entrata	entrance	**salotto**	living room

Memory practice

Fill in the blanks with the appropriate words and expressions. Do this from memory, and then go back and check your answers.

Questa casa è _____ piccola.

Ma ha una bella _____, due camere e un _____ grande.

Sì, e anche un salotto _____ e una sala da pranzo _____.

Il garage, _____, è un po' troppo piccolo.

Ma ha un'_____ assai grande!

Language notes

To form the imperative of **-ire** verbs, drop the **-ire** ending and add the following endings. Note that some verbs (as you know) require the change to **-isc**.

dormire (*to sleep*)

(tu) dorm**i** — *sleep (fam.)*

(Lei) dorm**a** — *sleep (pol.)*

(noi) dorm**iamo** — *let's sleep*

(voi) dorm**ite** — *sleep (pl.)*

(loro) dorm**ano** (dóhr-mah-noh) — *sleep (pol. pl.)*

finire (*to finish*)

(tu) fin**isci** — *finish (fam.)*

(Lei) fin**isca** — *finish (pol.)*

(noi) fin**iamo** — *let's finish*

(voi) fin**ite** — *finish (pl.)*

(loro) fin**iscano** (feeh-néehs-kah-noh) — *finish (pol. pl.)*

Dialogo

The house hunting continues:

MOGLIE: Se prendiamo questa casa, dobbiamo comprare tanti mobili nuovi.

If we get this house, we will have to buy a lot of new furniture.

MARITO: Sì, è vero, ma abbiamo già un bel divano e una poltrona bellisima.

Yes, it's true, but we already have a beautiful sofa and a very beautiful armchair.

MOGLIE: Sì, ma dobbiamo comprare un nuovo frigorifero e un nuovo tavolo per la sala da pranzo.

Yes, but we have to buy a new refrigerator and a new table for the dining room.

MARITO: D'accordo.

I agree.

MOGLIE: E anche un nuovo letto per la nostra camera.

And also a new bed for our bedroom.

MARITO: Forse conviene rimanere nel nostro condominio!

Maybe it is better to remain in our condo!

NEW VOCABULARY			
condominio	condo	**letto**	bed
convenire	to be better to	**mobile (móh-beeh-leh)**	piece of furniture
divano	sofa	**poltrona**	armchair
frigorifero (freeh-goh-réeh-feh-roh)	refrigerator	**rimanere**	to remain
		tanto	many, a lot
già	already	**tavolo (táh-voh-loh)**	table

Memory practice

Fill in the blanks with the appropriate words and expressions. Do this from memory, and then go back and check your answers.

Se prendiamo questa casa, dobbiamo comprare tanti _____ nuovi.

Sì, è vero, ma abbiamo _____ un bel _____ e una _____ bellisima.

Sì, ma dobbiamo comprare un nuovo _____ e un nuovo _____ per la sala da pranzo.

D'accordo.

E anche un nuovo _____ per la nostra _____.

Forse _____ rimanere nel nostro condominio!

Language notes

Note that **tanto** is a synonym of **molto**. And note that **convenire** is conjugated like **venire**.

EXERCISE
5·3

Tell the following people to do the indicated things.

1. Tell Giovanni to sleep.

_____

2. Tell Mr. Verdi to sleep.

_____

3. Tell Marco and Maria (together) to finish the coffee.

_____

4. Tell a group of young ladies to finish the book.

_____

5. Tell Bruna to finish the croissant.

_____

6. Tell Mrs. Verdi to finish the sandwich.

_____

7. Tell Marco and Maria (together) to sleep till (**fino a**) late.

_____

Carry out the following conversation tasks.

8. Say that this house is very small, but it has a beautiful kitchen, a beautiful bedroom, and a big bathroom.

_____

9. Say that the house has a magnificent living room and an exceptional dining room.

_____

10. Say that, however, the garage is very small.

_____

11. Say that the entrance is quite big.

_____

12. Say that you will have to buy many new pieces of furniture.

_____

13. Say that you already have a beautiful sofa and a beautiful armchair.

_____

14. Say that you want to buy a new refrigerator, a new bed for the bedroom, and a new table.

_____

15. Say that it is better to remain in your condo.

_____

Daily life

Shopping and banking are part of everyday life. Knowing how to converse in the relevant situations (at stores, at banks, and so on) is an obvious vital linguistic skill. This chapter will show you how to use that skill.

At the supermarket

Dialogo

Here's the kind of conversation that might take place at a supermarket, while shopping for food (**fare la spesa**):

COMMESSO: Quante mele desidera?	*How many apples do you want?*
CLIENTE: Una dozzina. Poi vorrei un mezzo chilo di quelle fragole.	*A dozen. Then I would like a half kilo of those strawberries.*
COMMESSO: Non prenda quelle! Queste sono più fresche.	*Don't take those! These are more fresh.*
CLIENTE: Vorrei anche dei piselli, dei fagioli e qualche pera.	*I would also like some peas, some beans, and a few pears.*
COMMESSO: Abbiamo anche delle pesche fresche.	*We also have some fresh peaches.*
CLIENTE: No, grazie. Basta così.	*No, thanks. This is enough.*

NEW VOCABULARY

bastare	to be enough	**fresco**	fresh
chilo	kilogram	**mela**	apple
desiderare	to desire, to want	**pera**	pear
dozzina	dozen	**pesca**	peach
fagiolo	bean	**pisello**	pea
fragola (fráh-goh-lah)	strawberry		

Memory practice

Fill in the blanks with the appropriate words and expressions. Do this from memory, and then go back and check your answers.

_____ mele desidera?

Una dozzina. Poi vorrei un mezzo chilo di quelle _____.

Non _____ quelle! Queste sono più fresche.

Vorrei anche dei piselli, dei fagioli e _____ pera.

Abbiamo anche _____ pesche fresche.

No, grazie. _____ così.

Language notes

Recall that **di** + definite article or **qualche** + singular noun allows you to express *some*, known technically as the partitive.

delle mele	*some apples*
qualche pera	*some pears*

Recall also that **quanto** is an adjective that changes according to the gender and number of the noun.

Quante mele?	*How many apples?*
Quanti piselli?	*How many peas?*

Note that **non prenda** is a negative imperative. As in all other cases, the negative is formed simply by putting **non** before the imperative verb. However, for the singular familiar (**tu**) form, the verb is changed to the infinitive.

	AFFIRMATIVE	NEGATIVE
Tu-forms:	Prendi! (*Take!*)	Non **prendere**! (*Don't take!*)
Lei-forms:	Prenda! (*Take!*)	Non prenda! (*Don't take!*)

Finally, here are the names of some common stores where food is sold:

il negozio di generi alimentari	*grocery/food store*
il panificio	*bakery*
il mercato	*market*
il supermercato	*supermarket*
la pizzicheria (peeh-tseeh-keh-réeh-ah)	*delicatessen*

Dialogo

Here is a similar conversation:

COMMESSA: Desidera, signore?	*May I help you, sir?*
CLIENTE: Vorrei dieci fette di prosciutto.	*I would like ten slices of prosciutto.*
COMMESSA: Il prosciutto che abbiamo è freschissimo. Altro?	*The prosciutto we have is very fresh. Anything else?*
CLIENTE: Un po' di salame.	*A bit of salami.*
COMMESSA: Abbiamo anche del formaggio buonissimo.	*We also have some very good cheese.*
CLIENTE: No, grazie. Va bene così.	*No thanks. That's it.*

fetta	slice	**prosciutto**	prosciutto ham
formaggio	cheese	**salame (*m.*)**	salami

Memory practice

Fill in the blanks with the appropriate words and expressions. Do this from memory, and then go back and check your answers.

_____, signore?

Vorrei dieci _____ di prosciutto.

Il prosciutto che abbiamo è _____. Altro?

Un po' di _____.

Abbiamo anche del _____ buonissimo.

No, grazie. Va bene _____.

Language notes

Note that the expression **Desidera?** is translated as *May I help you*? But, literally, it means *Do you want (something)?*

In previous chapters, you have come across irregular imperative verbs. Three of the most common are the following:

essere (*to be*)	**avere** (*to have*)	**fare** (*to do, to make*)
(tu) sii (*be*)	(tu) abbi (*have*)	(tu) fa' (*do*)
(Lei) sia (*be*)	(Lei) abbia (*have*)	(Lei) faccia (*do*)
(noi) siamo (*let's be*)	(noi) abbiamo (*let's have*)	(noi) facciamo (*let's do*)
(voi) siate (*be*)	(voi) abbiate (*have*)	(voi) fate (*do*)
(Loro) siano (*be*)	(Loro) abbiano (*have*)	(Loro) facciano (*do*)

And don't forget that the negative imperative of **tu**-forms is the infinitive.

Marco, fa' questo!	Marco, non fare questo!
Marco, do this!	*Marco, don't do this!*

Here are the names of some common food items, which will come in handy when shopping for food:

la carne	*meat*	il latte	*milk*
il pesce	*fish*	il vino	*wine*
il pane	*bread*	la frutta	*fruit*
l'acqua	*water*	la verdura	*vegetables*

Note that with these nouns, called mass nouns (because they have mainly a singular form), the partitive consists of **di** + singular definite article. The **qualche** form is never used with these nouns.

della carne	*some meat*
del pesce	*some fish*

As you know, adding **-issimo** to the end of an adjective translates as *very*.

bellissimo   *very beautiful*

freschissimo   *very fresh*

Note that the hard **c** of adjectives like **fresco** is retained by adding an **h**.

EXERCISE
6·1

Say that you want some of each item mentioned.

EXAMPLE: mele   *Vorrei delle mele.*

1. fragole _____

2. piselli _____

3. pere _____

4. pesche _____

5. fagioli _____

6. formaggio _____

7. prosciutto _____

8. carne _____

9. pesce _____

10. pane _____

11. acqua _____

12. latte _____

13. vino _____

14. frutta _____

15. verdura _____

Put the following commands in the negative. Remember to use the infinitive for **tu***-forms.*

EXAMPLE: Signora, prenda queste mele!

               Signora, non prenda queste mele!

16. Maria, torna domani!

_____

17. Signor Marchi, faccia questo!

_____

18. Marco, fa' quella domanda al professore!

_____

19. Giovanni e Bruna, siate vivaci!

   _____

20. Maria, abbi fretta (*hurry*)!

   _____

Carry out the following conversation tasks.

21. Ask someone how many strawberries they would like.

   _____

22. Say that you would like a dozen (**dozzina di**) apples and a kilogram of peaches.

   _____

23. Say that these strawberries are more fresh.

   _____

24. Say "This is enough."

   _____

25. As a store employee, ask a customer if you can help him/her.

   _____

26. Say that you would like a dozen slices of prosciutto.

   _____

27. Say that you would also like a bit of salami.

   _____

28. Say that the cheese is very good and very fresh.

   _____

29. Say that you want to buy some prosciutto at the delicatessen on National Street.

   _____

30. Say that you want to buy some bread at the bakery on Dante Street.

   _____

Shopping

Dialogo

The following conversation is characteristic of what one would say at a women's clothing store while shopping (**fare delle spese**):

COMMESSA: Buongiorno. Mi dica!	*Good day. May I help you?* (literally: *Tell me!*)
CLIENTE: Vorrei una giacca alla moda.	*I would like a fashionable jacket.*
COMMESSA: Che taglia porta?	*What's your size?*

CLIENTE: Il quarantadue.		*I'm a 42.*
COMMESSA: Vuole provarsi questa?		*Would you like to try this one on?*
CLIENTE: Sì. Ha dei pantaloni che vanno insieme?		*Yes. Do you have pants that go together?*
COMMESSA: Sì, questi azzurri.		*Yes, these blue ones.*
CLIENTE: Belli! Dov'è il camerino?		*Beautiful! Where's the changing room?*
COMMESSA: Vada lì, a destra.		*Go there, to the right.*

NEW VOCABULARY

alla moda	in style, fashionable	**pantaloni** (*m., pl.*)	pants
camerino	changing room	**portare**	to wear
giacca	jacket	**provarsi (provare + si)**	to try on
insieme	together	**taglia**	size

Memory practice

Fill in the blanks with the appropriate words and expressions. Do this from memory, and then go back and check your answers.

Buongiorno. Mi _____!

Vorrei una giacca _____.

Che _____ porta?

Il quarantadue.

Vuole _____ questa?

Sì. Ha dei _____ che vanno insieme?

Sì, questi _____.

Belli! Dov'è il _____?

_____ lì, a destra.

Language notes

The forms **vada** and **dica** are imperatives of **andare** and **dire**, irregular verbs that you have come across in previous chapters. Another common verb that is irregular in the imperative is **venire**. Here are their conjugations:

andare (*to go*)	**dire** (*to say, to tell*)	**venire** (*to come*)
(tu) va' (*go*)	(tu) di' (*tell*)	(tu) vieni (*come*)
(Lei) vada (*go*)	(Lei) dica (*tell*)	(Lei) venga (*come*)
(noi) andiamo (*let's go*)	(noi) diciamo (*let's tell*)	(noi) veniamo (*let's come*)
(voi) andate (*go*)	(voi) dite (*tell*)	(voi) venite (*come*)
(loro) vadano (*go*)	(loro) dicano (*tell*)	(loro) vengano (*come*)

Here are the names of some common colors in Italian. These will come in handy when shopping for clothes. Recall that **blu** is an invariable adjective. So are **arancione**, **marrone**, and **viola**. They never change in form, no matter what the gender and number of the noun they modify.

arancione (*inv.*)	*orange*	marrone (*inv.*)	*brown*
azzurro	*blue*	nero	*black*
bianco	*white*	rosso	*red*
giallo	*yellow*	verde	*green*
grigio	*gray*	viola (*inv.*)	*purple*

And here are the name of some common clothing items:

il vestito	*dress*	la camicia	*shirt*
la gonna	*skirt*	la cravatta	*tie*
la camicetta	*blouse*	l'abito	*suit*
la cintura	*belt*	la borsa	*purse*
la maglia	*sweater*		

Dialogo

Now let's put the spotlight on a conversation in a footwear store:

COMMESSO: Desidera, signore?	*May I help you, sir?*
CLIENTE: Quanto costano questi stivali?	*How much do these boots cost?*
COMMESSO: Duecento euro. Sono in saldo.	*Two hundred euros. They're on sale.*
CLIENTE: E queste scarpe?	*And these shoes?*
COMMESSO: Costano trecento euro.	*They cost three hundred euros.*
CLIENTE: Posso provarle?	*May I try them on?*
COMMESSO: Certo. Che numero porta?	*Of course. What's your size (literally, number)?*
CLIENTE: Il trentotto.	*Size thirty-eight.*
COMMESSO: Le stanno proprio bene!	*They really look good on you!*

NEW VOCABULARY

in saldo	on sale	**stare bene**	to look good on
scarpa	shoe	**stivale**	boot

Memory practice

Fill in the blanks with the appropriate words and expressions. Do this from memory, and then go back and check your answers.

Desidera, signore?

Quanto costano questi _____?

Duecento euro. Sono _____.

E queste _____?

_____ trecento euro.

Posso provarle?

Certo. Che _____ porta?

Il trentotto.

Le _____ proprio _____!

Language notes

In the previous chapter, you learned to form and use first-conjugation verbs in the present perfect. Recall that the verbs discussed were conjugated with **avere** as the auxiliary and that the past participle was formed by changing -**are** to -**ato**, for example:

(io) ho lavorato	*I have worked, I worked*
(tu) hai cercato	*you have searched, you searched*

and so on.

The same pattern applies to second- and third-conjugation verbs. In the case of the second conjugation, the past participle is formed by replacing -**ere** with -**uto**, and in the case of the third conjugation, by replacing -**ire** with -**ito**. Here are **credere** and **finire** completely conjugated:

credere (*to believe*)

(io) ho creduto	*I have believed, I believed*
(tu) hai creduto	*you have believed, you believed* (fam.)
(Lei) ha creduto	*you have believed, you believed* (pol.)
(lui) ha creduto	*he has believed, he believed*
(lei) ha creduto	*she has believed, she believed*
(noi) abbiamo creduto	*we have believed, we believed*
(voi) avete creduto	*you have believed, you believed* (pl.)
(loro) hanno creduto	*they have believed, they believed*

finire (*to finish*)

(io) ho finito	*I have finished, I finished*
(tu) hai finito	*you have finished, you finished* (fam.)
(Lei) ha finito	*you have finished, you finished* (pol.)
(lui) ha finito	*he has finished, he finished*
(lei) ha finito	*she has finished, she finished*
(noi) abbiamo finito	*we have finished, we finished*
(voi) avete finito	*you have finished, you finished* (pl.)
(loro) hanno finito	*they have finished, they finished*

EXERCISE
6·2

Tell the following people to do the things indicated.

EXAMPLE: Tell Maria to go downtown.

Maria, va' in centro!

1. Tell Professor Giusto (*a male*) to go downtown.

_____

2. Tell Marco and Bruna to go downtown.

_____

3. Tell Maria to tell the truth (**la verità**).

_____

4. Tell Dr. Marinelli (*a female*) to tell the truth.

_____

5. Tell Giovanni and Maria to tell the truth.

_____

6. Tell Marco to come here.

_____

7. Tell Mrs. Martini to come here.

_____

8. Tell Marco and Maria to come here.

_____

Say that you bought the following yesterday.

EXAMPLE: an orange dress and a blue skirt

Ieri ho comprato un vestito arancione e una gonna azzurra.

9. a white blouse and a yellow belt

_____

10. two gray sweaters and a brown shirt

_____

11. a purple tie, a red purse, a green suit, and a black jacket

_____

Say that the following people did not do the indicated things.

EXAMPLE: (tu) finire di leggere quel libro

(Tu) non hai finito di leggere quel libro.

12. (il professore) avere tempo (*time*)

_____

13. (noi) dovere comprare quell'abito

_____

14. (voi) potere comprare quegli stivali

_____

15. (tu) volere leggere quel libro

_____

16. (io) capire la verità

_____

17. (tu) dormire fino a tardi

_____

18. (il ragazzo) preferire il cornetto

_____

19. (noi) finire di lavorare (*working*)

_____

20. (voi) capire il libro

_____

Carry out the following conversation tasks.

21. Say that you would like to buy a jacket in style.

_____

22. Ask someone (*politely*) what his or her (*clothing*) size is.

_____

23. Ask someone (*politely*) if she wants to try on a blue dress.

_____

24. Say that you would like pants that go together with the green jacket.

_____

25. Ask where the changing room is.

_____

26. Tell someone (*politely*) to go there, to the right.

_____

27. Ask a store clerk how much the boots and the shoes cost.

_____

28. Say that the shoes are on sale.

_____

29. Ask someone (*politely*) what his/her shoe size is.

_____

30. Tell someone (*politely*) that they (*the shoes*) look really good on him/her.

_____

Banking

Dialogo

Here's what a typical conversation in a bank might sound like:

IMPIEGATO:	Che cosa desidera, signorina?	*May I help you with something, Miss?*
SIGNORINA:	Vorrei depositare questi soldi nel mio conto.	*I would like to deposit this money in my account.*
IMPIEGATO:	Altro?	*Anything else?*
SIGNORINA:	Vorrei prelevare del denaro da quest'altro conto.	*I would like to withdraw some money from this other account.*
IMPIEGATO:	Quanto?	*How much?*
SIGNORINA:	Cinquecento euro, per favore.	*Five hundred euros, please.*
IMPIEGATO:	EccoLe! Firmi questo modulo.	*Here you are. Sign this form.*
SIGNORINA:	Grazie.	*Thank you.*

NEW VOCABULARY

conto	account	**firmare**	to sign
denaro	money	**modulo (móh-dooh-loh)**	form
depositare	to deposit	**prelevare**	to withdraw

Memory practice

Fill in the blanks with the appropriate words and expressions. Do this from memory, and then go back and check your answers.

Che cosa _____, signorina?

Vorrei _____ questi soldi nel mio _____.

Altro??

Vorrei _____ del _____ da quest'altro conto.

Quanto?

Cinquecento _____, per favore.

EccoLe! _____ questo modulo.

Grazie.

Language notes

So far you have been working with verbs conjugated with **avere** as the auxiliary in the present perfect. There are a small number of verbs, however, that are conjugated with **essere**. The best way to determine which verbs are conjugated with **essere** is to look it up. In this book this fact will be shown with (**ess.**) when the verb is first introduced and in the glossary. Of the verbs you have come across so far, the following are conjugated with **essere: andare, bastare, costare, convenire, diventare, essere, piacere, rimanere, sembrare, stare, tornare, venire.**

In this case, the past participle agrees with the subject (**io**, **tu**, and so on), as if it were an adjective.

Marco è andat**o** in centro ieri.	*Marco went downtown yesterday.*
Maria è andat**a** in centro ieri.	*Maria went downtown yesterday.*

Here is **andare** fully conjugated for you in the present perfect:

andare (*to go*)	
(io) sono andato (-a)	*I have gone, I went*
(tu) sei andato (-a)	*you have gone, you went* (fam.)
(Lei) è andato (-a)	*you have gone, you went* (pol.)
(lui) è andato	*he has gone, he went*
(lei) è andata	*she has gone, she went*
(noi) siamo andati (-e)	*we have gone, we went*
(voi) siete andati (-e)	*you have gone, you went* (pl.)
(loro) sono andati (-e)	*they have gone, they went*

Dialogo

The bank conversation continues:

Impiegato:	Come le vuole?	*How would you like them (the money)?*
Signorina:	In biglietti di taglio piccolo.	*In small bills.*
Impiegato:	Va bene. Ha bisogno di altro?	*OK. Do you need anything else?*
Signorina:	Mi può cambiare in spiccioli questo biglietto?	*Can you change this bill into small change?*
Impiegato:	Certo!	*Of course.*

NEW VOCABULARY			
biglietto	bill	**spicciolo**	coin, small change
cambiare	to change, to exchange	**taglio piccolo**	small

Memory practice

Fill in the blanks with the appropriate words and expressions. Do this from memory, and then go back and check your answers.

Come le _____?

In biglietti di _____ piccolo.

Va bene. Ha _____ di altro?

Mi può _____ in _____ questo biglietto?

Language notes

As you know, the present perfect (and all compound tenses) are formed with an auxiliary verb and the past participle. Needless to say, some verbs have irregular past participles. Of the verbs you have come across so far, the following have irregular past participles:

VERB	PAST PARTICIPLE
chiedere	chiesto
convenire	convenuto
dire	detto
essere	stato
fare	fatto
leggere	letto
prendere	preso
rimanere	rimasto
stare	stato
vedere	visto
venire	venuto

EXERCISE
6·3

Say that the following people did not do the indicated things.

EXAMPLE: (tu) andare in centro

(Tu) non sei andato (-a) in centro. [Note: the **tu** can be either a male or female, hence the need to show both endings in the past participle.]

1. (io) andare al supermercato

_____

2. (tu) venire con loro in centro

_____

3. (quell'uomo) tornare dal centro

_____

4. (quella donna) tornare dal centro

_____

5. (noi) stare in Italia

_____

6. (voi) venire in centro

_____

7. (gli studenti) rimanere in classe (*in class*)

_____

8. (le donne) essere al bar

_____

9. (quegli stivali) costare molto

_____

10. (quelle scarpe) costare tanto

_____

11. (Marco) chiedere quelle domande al professore

_____

12. (Maria) dire la verità

_____

13. (io) fare la spesa ieri

_____

14. (mio fratello) leggere quel libro

_____

15. (io) prendere il caffè al bar

_____

16. (tu) vedere Maria ieri

_____

17. (loro) venire con noi

_____

Carry out the following conversation tasks.

18. Say that you would like to deposit some money in your account.

_____

19. Say that you would like to withdraw some money from your other account.

_____

20. Tell someone (*politely*) to sign this form.

_____

21. Say that you want small bills.

_____

22. Ask the teller (*politely, of course*) to change these bills into small change.

_____

Weather, seasons, and holidays

The weather, the change of seasons, and, of course, holidays are common topics in conversation. This chapter will show you how to carry out conversations in this area of everyday life.

Weather

Dialogo

The following conversation is all about the weather:

AMICO:	Fa troppo freddo!	*It's too cold.*
AMICA:	Ma c'è un bel sole e non tira vento.	*But there's a beautiful sun, and it's not windy.*
AMICO:	Preferisco andare al mare.	*I prefer going to the sea.*
AMICA:	Non io. Preferisco la montagna.	*Not I. I prefer the mountains.*
AMICO:	Ma nevica sempre d'inverno.	*But it always snows in the winter.*
AMICA:	Non sei mai contento!	*You're never happy!*
AMICO:	Neanche tu!	*Nor are you!*

NEW VOCABULARY

contento	happy, content	**nevicare**	to snow
freddo	cold	**sole** (*m.*)	sun
inverno	winter	**tirare vento**	to be windy
mare (*m.*)	sea	**vento**	wind
montagna	mountain(s)		

Memory practice

Fill in the blanks with the appropriate words and expressions. Do this from memory, and then go back and check your answers.

_____ troppo freddo!

Ma c'è un bel sole e non _____ vento.

Preferisco andare al _____.

Non io. Preferisco la _____.

Ma _____ sempre d'inverno.

Non sei mai _____ !

_____ tu!

Language notes

Italian uses double negatives in sentence construction. This simply means that **non** is used with adverbs such as **mai** (*ever*) to produce *never*. Here are the most common double negatives:

non… mai	*never*
non… più	*no more, no longer*
non… niente	*nothing*
(*also*: non… nulla)	
non… neanche	*neither*
non… nessuno	*no one*
non… né… né	*neither . . . nor*

The **non** is dropped when used at the beginning of a sentence, or for emphasis.

Neanche tu!   *Nor (neither) you!*

Note the use of **fare** with weather expressions: **fare freddo** (*to be cold*), **fare caldo** (*to be hot*).

Dialogo

The previous conversation continues:

Amico:	Andiamo in centro oggi, va bene?	*Let's go downtown today, OK?*
Amica:	Non vedi che piove forte?	*Don't you see that it's raining hard?*
Amico:	Non importa. Fa caldo e ho voglia di uscire.	*It doesn't matter. It's warm, and I feel like going out.*
Amica:	Va bene. Andiamo al cinema.	*OK. Let's go to the movies.*
Amico:	D'accordo.	*I agree.*

NEW VOCABULARY

avere voglia di	to feel like	**forte**	strong, hard
caldo	hot, warm	**piovere** (pyóh-veh-reh)	to rain
cinema (*m., inv.*)	cinema, movies	**uscire** (ess.)	to go out

Memory practice

Fill in the blanks with the appropriate words and expressions. Do this from memory, and then go back and check your answers.

_____ in centro oggi, va bene?

Non vedi che _____ forte.

Non importa. Fa _____ e ho _____ di uscire.

Va bene. Andiamo al _____.
D'accordo.

Language notes

In this and previous chapters, you have come across object pronouns (*me, him, her,* and so on).
The time has come to learn them formally. Here are the direct object pronouns in Italian:

me	mi
you (fam., sing.)	ti
you (pol., sing.)	La
him	lo
her	la
us	ci
you (fam., pl.)	vi
them (m.)	li
them (f.)	le

Note that in a sentence these come before the verb.

Marco **mi** chiama ogni sera.	*Marco calls **me** every night.*
Maria, chi **ti** chiama spesso?	*Maria, who calls **you** often?*
Signorina, chi **La** chiama spesso?	*Miss, who calls **you** often?*
Il professore **lo** chiama spesso.	*The professor calls **him** often.*
Lui non **la** chiama mai.	*He never calls **her**.*
Marco **ci** aspetta.	*Marco is waiting **for us**.*
Maria non **vi** capisce.	*Maria does not understand **you**.*
Io non **li** conosco.	*I do not know **them** (m.).*
Lui non **le** conosce.	*He does not know **them** (f.).*

The verb **uscire** (*to go out*) is found in this dialogue. It is a very useful verb, and it is irregular.
Here are its present indicative forms:

(io) esco	*I am going out*
(tu) esci	*you are going out* (fam.)
(Lei) esce	*you are going out* (pol.)
(lui) esce	*he is going out*
(lei) esce	*she is going out*
(noi) usciamo	*we are going out*
(voi) uscite	*you are going out* (pl.)
(loro) escono (éhs-koh-noh)	*they are going out*

Now, here are its imperative forms:

(tu) esci	*go out* (fam.)
(Lei) esca	*go out* (pol.)
(noi) usciamo	*let's go out*
(voi) uscite	*go out* (pl.)
(loro) escano (éhs-kah-noh)	*go out* (pol. pl.)

Finally, note that it is conjugated with **essere** in the present perfect:

Io sono uscito (-a) ieri.	*I went out yesterday.*
Mio fratello è uscito con Bruna.	*My brother went out with Bruna.*
Mia sorella non è uscita ieri.	*My sister did not go out yesterday.*

EXERCISE
7·1

Rewrite each statement in the negative.

EXAMPLE: Marco conosce tutti.

Marco non conosce nessuno.

1. Il tuo amico va sempre al cinema.

_____

2. La sua amica sa tutto.

_____

3. Loro vanno ancora in montagna.

_____

4. Maria conosce tutti.

_____

5. Io voglio la carne e il pesce.

_____

Using appropriate direct object pronouns, identify the people Maria never calls.

EXAMPLE: me

Maria non mi chiama mai.

6. you (*fam., sing.*)

_____

7. us

_____

8. you (*pl.*)

_____

9. him

_____

10. her

_____

11. them (*all males*)

_____

12. them (*all females*)

_____

Translate the following sentences into Italian.

13. I never go out.

_____

14. The girls have gone out already.

_____

15. Marco, go out with Maria!

_____

16. Mrs. Verdi, go out with your husband!

_____

17. My brother went out a few moments ago.

_____

18. Marco, do you often go out?

_____

Carry out the following conversation tasks.

19. Say that it's too cold.

_____

20. Now say that it's too hot.

_____

21. Say that you prefer to go to the mountains rather than (**piuttosto che**) to the sea.

_____

22. Say that it always snows in the winter.

_____

23. Tell someone (*informally*) that he/she is never happy.

_____

24. Tell a friend to go downtown with you.

_____

25. Say that you do not want to go downtown because it is raining hard.

_____

26. Say that you feel like going out.

_____

27. Suggest to someone to go to the movies (*together*).

_____

Seasons

Dialogo

The next conversation involves talking about the seasons:

AMICA:	Amo la primavera e l'autunno, e tu?	*I love spring and fall, and you?*
AMICO:	Io preferisco l'estate perché amo il caldo.	*I prefer summer because I love the heat.*
AMICA:	A primavera sbocciano le piante.	*In spring, the plants blossom.*
AMICO:	Come il mio amore per te.	*Like my love for you.*
AMICA:	Sei sempre romantico!	*You are always romantic!*

NEW VOCABULARY

amare	to love		**primavera**	spring
amore (*m.*)	love		**romantico**	romantic
autunno	autumn, fall		**(roh-máhn-teeh-koh)**	
estate (*f.*)	summer		**sbocciare**	to blossom
pianta	plant			

Memory practice

Fill in the blanks with the appropriate words and expressions. Do this from memory, and then go back and check your answers.

Amo la _____ e l'autunno, e tu?

Io preferisco l'_____ perché amo il caldo.

A primavera _____ le piante.

Come il mio _____ per te.

Sei sempre _____!

Language notes

Let's continue with the object pronouns. Here are the indirect object pronouns (*to me, to her, to him*, and so on).

to me	mi
to you (fam., sing.)	ti
to you (pol., sing.)	Le
to him	gli
to her	le
to us	ci
to you (fam., pl.)	vi
to them (m.)	gli
to them (f.)	gli

Note that these also come before the verb. As you can see, you will have to be very careful when using these pronouns at first, until you become familiar with them.

Marco **mi** ha detto la verità.	*Marco told **me** the truth.*
Maria, che cosa **ti** ha detto lui?	*Maria, what did he say **to you**?*
Signorina, che cosa **Le** ha detto lui?	*Miss, what did he say **to you**?*
Il professore non **gli** ha detto la verità.	*The professor did not tell **him** the truth.*
Lui non **le** ha mandato un messaggino.	*He did not send a text **to her**.*
Marco **ci** ha mandato un messaggino.	*Marco sent a text **to us**.*
Maria non **vi** ha detto tutto.	*Maria did not tell **you** everything.*
Io non **gli** ho parlato.	*I did not speak **to them** (m./f.).*

Dialogo

The previous conversation continues:

AMICO:	Odio l'inverno e il freddo, e tu?	*I hate winter and the cold, and you?*
AMICA:	Io invece lo amo, perché mi piace la neve.	*I, instead, love it, because I like the snow.*
AMICO:	Non io. Ma mi piace molto l'autunno.	*Not I, but I really like the fall.*
AMICA:	Perché cadono le foglie?	*Because the leaves fall?*
AMICO:	Come il tuo amore per me?	*Like your love for me?*

NEW VOCABULARY

cadere (ess.)	to fall		**neve** (*f.*)	snow
foglia	leaf		**odiare**	to hate
invece	instead			

Memory practice

Fill in the blanks with the appropriate words and expressions. Do this from memory, and then go back and check your answers.

_____ l'inverno e il freddo, e tu?

Io _____ lo amo, perché mi piace la _____.

Non io. Ma mi piace molto l'_____.

Perché cadono le _____?

Come il tuo _____ per me?

Language notes

Sometimes, you might need to use stressed pronouns in place of the ones discussed above. These come after the verb for emphasis. And they are the only ones possible after prepositions.

me	me
you (fam., sing.)	te
you (pol., sing.)	Lei
him	lui
her	lei
us	noi
you (fam., pl.)	voi
them (m.)	loro
them (f.)	loro
Marco ha chiamato me, non te!	*Marco called me, not you!*
Venite con noi, va bene?	*Come with us, OK?*
Lui parla a me spesso.	*He talks to me often.*
Noi parliamo di lei spesso.	*We speak of her often.*

EXERCISE
7·2

Using appropriate indirect object pronouns, identify the people Maria has not spoken to.

EXAMPLE: to me

Maria non mi ha parlato.

1. to you (*fam., sing.*)

_____

2. to us

_____

3. to you (*pl.*)

_____

4. to him

_____

5. to her

_____

6. to them (*all males*)

_____

7. to them (*all females*)

_____

Now, using appropriate stressed object pronouns, identify the people with whom Maria went out or to whom she spoke as indicated.

EXAMPLE: **me**/uscire

Maria è uscita con me.

me/parlare

Maria ha parlato a me.

8. **you** (*fam., sing.*)/uscire

_____

9. **us**/parlare

_____

10. **you** (*pl.*)/uscire

_____

11. **him**/parlare

_____

12. **her**/uscire

_____

13. **them** (*all males*)/parlare

_____

14. **them** (*all females*)/uscire

_____

Carry out the following conversation tasks.

15. Say that you love the spring, but that you hate winter.

_____

16. Say that you prefer summer because you love the heat.

_____

17. Say that in the spring the plants are in bloom.

_____

18. Tell your romantic partner that he/she is romantic.

_____

19. Say that your love for him/her is very strong (**forte**).

_____

20. Say that you like the snow.

_____

21. Say that you love autumn because the leaves fall.

_____

Holidays

Dialogo

The following conversation deals with major holidays in Italy:

AMICA:	È già Natale!	_It's already Christmas!_
AMICO:	Io amo le feste natalizie, e tu?	_I love the Christmas holidays, and you?_
AMICA:	Io preferisco la Pasqua.	_I prefer Easter._
AMICO:	Perché?	_Why?_
AMICA:	Fa bel tempo e tutto comincia a crescere.	_The weather is beautiful, and everything begins to grow._

NEW VOCABULARY

crescere (kréh-sheh-reh)	to grow	natalizio	of Christmas
festa	feast, holiday, party	Pasqua	Easter
Natale (*m.*)	Christmas	tempo	weather

Memory practice

Fill in the blanks with the appropriate words and expressions. Do this from memory, and then go back and check your answers.

È già _____!

Io amo le _____ natalizie, e tu?

Io preferisco la _____.

Perché?

Fa _____ tempo e tutto comincia a crescere.

Language notes

The object pronouns **lo**, **la**, **li**, and **le** also stand for things and are thus translated as *it* and *they*. As you know by now, the pronoun form agrees in gender and number with the noun phrase it replaces.

Compro **il romanzo** domani.	*I am buying **the novel** tomorrow.*
Lo compro domani.	*I am buying **it** tomorrow.*
Compro **quegli stivali** domani.	*I am buying **those boots** tomorrow.*
Li compro domani.	*I am buying **them** tomorrow.*
Non prendo **quella giacca**.	*I am not taking **that jacket**.*
Non **la** prendo.	*I am not taking **it**.*
La mia amica non vuole **le scarpe**.	*My friend doesn't want **the shoes**.*
La mia amica non **le** vuole.	*My friend doesn't want **them**.*

One more thing. If the verb is in the present perfect (or any other compound tense), then the past participle agrees with the preceding pronoun.

Ho comprato **il romanzo** ieri.	*I bought **the novel** yesterday.*
Lo ho (l'ho) comprat**o** ieri.	*I bought **it** yesterday.*
Ho comprato **quegli stivali** ieri.	*I bought **those boots** yesterday.*
Li ho comprat**i** ieri.	*I bought **them** yesterday.*
Non ho preso **quella giacca**.	*I didn't take **that jacket**.*
Non **la** ho (l'ho) pres**a**.	*I didn't take **it**.*
La mia amica non ha voluto **le scarpe**.	*My friend didn't want **the shoes**.*
La mia amica non **le** ha volut**e**.	*My friend didn't want **them**.*

Dialogo

The previous conversation continues:

AMICA: È già Ferragosto!	*It's already Ferragosto (August 15)!*
AMICO: Vero. Tutti vanno in vacanza.	*True. Everybody's going on vacation.*
AMICA: Sì, ma purtroppo io devo lavorare.	*Yes, but unfortunately, I have to work.*
AMICO: Non importa. Quando vai in ferie andiamo in vacanza anche noi.	*It doesn't matter. We'll also go on vacation when you are off.*
AMICA: Sei un vero amico!	*You're a real friend!*

NEW VOCABULARY

in ferie	on vacation, off work	**vacanza**	vacation
purtroppo	unfortunately		

Memory practice

Fill in the blanks with the appropriate words and expressions. Do this from memory, and then go back and check your answers.

È _____ Ferragosto!

Vero. Tutti vanno in _____.

Sì, ma _____ io devo lavorare.

Non importa. Quando vai in _____ andiamo in vacanza anche noi.

Sei un _____ amico!

Language notes

Sometimes, the direct and indirect pronouns are required in the same sentence. In that case, the indirect pronouns come first and are changed as follows:

mi	*is changed to*	me
ti	*is changed to*	te
gli	*is changed to*	glie
le	*is changed to*	glie
ci	*is changed to*	ce
vi	*is changed to*	ve

Note that the only direct object pronouns used in double pronoun constructions are **lo**, **la**, **li**, and **le**. All double pronouns are written as separate words, except the ones formed with **glie**, which are written as single words.

Marco **mi** dice sempre **la verità**.	*Marco always tells **me the truth**.*
Marco **me la** dice sempre.	*Marco always tells **it to me**.*
Maria **gli** dice sempre **la verità**.	*Maria always tells **him the truth**.*
Maria **gliela** dice sempre.	*Maria always tells **it to him**.*
Io ho comprato **le scarpe a mia sorella**.	*I bought **my sister the shoes**.*
Io **gliele** ho comprate.	*I bought **them for her**. [Recall that the past participle agrees with lo, la, li, le.]*
Nostro padre **ci** ha comprato **gli stivali**.	*Our father bought **us the boots**.*
Nostro padre **ce li** ha comprati.	*Our father bought **them for us**.*

EXERCISE
7·3

*Replace each phrase in italics with the appropriate direct object pronoun (**lo**, **la**, **li**, **le**), rewriting the sentence and making any necessary changes.*

EXAMPLE: Marco ha comprato *gli stivali* ieri.

Marco li ha comprati ieri.

1. Io ho preso *l'espresso* a quel bar.

2. Noi abbiamo letto *quel romanzo* già.

   _____

3. Mia sorella ha comprato *le scarpe nuove* ieri.

   _____

4. La sua amica ha fatto *la spesa* ieri.

   _____

5. Mia cugina non ha voluto *i pantaloni nuovi*.

   _____

6. Non ho ancora finito *quel libro*.

   _____

7. Maria non ha mai detto *la verità*.

   _____

8. Ho finito *i piselli*.

   _____

9. Non ho mai preferito *le mele*.

   _____

*Now replace the italicized direct object with an appropriate pronoun (**lo, la, li, le**), and then rewrite the whole sentence, making the necessary adjustments. Note that you will have to use double pronouns throughout.*

EXAMPLE: Maria mi ha detto *la verità*.

   Maria me la ha (l'ha) detta.

10. Io ti ho comprato *i cornetti*.

   _____

11. Mio fratello gli ha chiesto *le domande* ieri.

   _____

12. Mio fratello le ha comprato *gli stivali nuovi* ieri.

   _____

13. Tu ci hai mandato *i messaggini*, vero?

   _____

14. Io vi ho preso *un caffè*, va bene?

   _____

Carry out the following conversation tasks.

15. Say that it is already Christmas.

   _____

16. Say that you love the Christmas holidays.

   _____

17. Say that you do not like Easter because it is always raining.

   _____

18. Say that you love spring because the weather is beautiful and everything starts to grow.

   _____

19. Say that everyone goes on vacation in August.

   _____

20. Say that unfortunately you have to work.

   _____

21. Tell someone that he/she is a real friend.

   _____

Leisure time

Enjoying sports and going out, especially to restaurants, is part of modern-day life. This chapter is all about that.

Sports

Dialogo

The following conversation deals with sports:

FRATELLO: Ti piace sciare?	*Do you like skiing?*
SORELLA: No! Preferisco il nuoto o il tennis.	*No, I prefer swimming or tennis.*
FRATELLO: C'è una piscina qui vicino.	*There's a pool near here.*
SORELLA: Andiamoci questo pomeriggio!	*Let's go this afternoon!*
FRATELLO: Non posso! C'è il campionato di calcio alla TV!	*I can't! The soccer championship is on TV!*
SORELLA: Uffa! Io vado da sola!	*Ugh! I'm going by myself!*

NEW VOCABULARY

campionato	championship, playoffs	**televisione** (*f.*)	television
nuoto	swimming	**tennis**	tennis
piscina	swimming pool	**TV** (*f.*)	TV
sciare (sheeh-áh-reh)	to ski		

Memory practice

Fill in the blanks with the appropriate words and expressions. Do this from memory, and then go back and check your answers.

Ti piace _____?

No! Preferisco il _____ o il tennis.

C'è una _____ qui vicino.

Andiamoci questo _____!

Non posso! C'è il _____ di calcio alla TV!

Uffa! Io vado da _____!

Language notes

Except for the stressed pronouns, you learned in Chapter 7 that the object pronouns go before the verb. An exception is in the imperative. In this case, they are attached to the familiar forms (**tu**, **noi**, **voi**).

Tu forms

Marco, compra quell'abito!	*Marco, buy that suit!*
Marco, compralo!	*Marco, buy it!*
Maria, finisci la carne!	*Maria, finish the meat!*
Maria, finiscila!	*Maria, finish it!*
Giovanni, parla al professore!	*Giovanni, speak to the professor!*
Giovanni parlagli!	*Giovanni, speak to him!*

Noi forms

Compriamo quelle scarpe!	*Let's buy those shoes!*
Compriamole!	*Let's buy them!*
Finiamo i piselli!	*Let's finish the peas!*
Finiamoli!	*Let's finish them!*
Parliamo alla sua amica!	*Let's speak to his friend!*
Parliamole!	*Let's speak to her!*

Voi forms

Comprate quelle scarpe!	*Buy those shoes!*
Compratele!	*Buy them!*
Finite il pesce!	*Finish the fish!*
Finitelo!	*Finish it!*

Recall that in the negative imperative, the **tu**-form uses the infinitive. To add on the pronoun, drop the -**e** of the infinitive.

Marco, non comprare quell'abito!	*Marco, don't buy that suit!*
Marco, non comprarlo!	*Marco, don't buy it!*
Maria, non finire la carne!	*Maria, don't finish the meat!*
Maria, non finirla!	*Maria, don't finish it!*

Note that when you attach the pronoun, you retain the word stress of the verb as it was before the add-on.

Finiscila = (feeh-néeh-sheeh-lah)

With the polite forms (**Lei**, **Loro**), the pronoun goes before the verb.

Lei forms

Signor Verdi, compri quell'abito!	*Mr. Verdi, buy that suit!*
Signor Verdi, lo compri!	*Mr. Verdi, buy it!*
Signora, finisca la carne!	*Madam, finish the meat!*
Signora, la finisca!	*Madam, finish it!*

Loro forms

Comprino quelle scarpe!	*Buy those shoes!*
Le comprino!	*Buy them!*
Finiscano il pesce!	*Finish the fish!*
Lo finiscano!	*Finish it!*

Here are some useful words for sports:

l'atletica leggera	*track and field*	la pallacanestro	*basketball*
l'automobilismo	*car racing*	il pattinaggio	*skating*
il calcio	*soccer*	il pugilato	*boxing*
la lotta	*wrestling*		

Dialogo

The next conversation deals with going to the gym and working out:

AMICA:	Volevi venire con me in palestra?	*Did you want to come with me to the gym?*
AMICO:	No. Preferisco fare il footing.	*No. I prefer jogging.*
AMICA:	Ma non ti piace la pallacanestro?	*But don't you like basketball?*
AMICO:	Sì, ma non ho un buon partner.	*Yes, but I don't have a good partner.*
AMICA:	Capisco.	*I understand.*

NEW VOCABULARY

fare il footing   to jog   **palestra**   gym

Memory practice

Fill in the blanks with the appropriate words and expressions. Do this from memory, and then go back and check your answers.

_____ venire con me in palestra?

No. Preferisco _____ il footing.

Ma non ti piace la _____?

Sì, ma non ho un _____ partner.

Capisco.

Language notes

The verb form **volevi** in the dialogue is in the imperfect tense. This is the tense that is generally translated as *I used to do something* or *I was doing something*. It indicates that the action in the past went on for a while, never ended, or was part of a state (such as having blond hair).

To form the imperfect in Italian, drop the **-re** of all three conjugations and add on the same set of endings: **-vo**, **-vi**, **-va**, **-vamo**, **-vate**, **-vano**. Here are three verbs—**andare**, **leggere**, and **finire**—fully conjugated for you, representing the first, second, and third conjugations, respectively.

andare (*to go*)

(io) andavo	*I used to go, I was going*
(tu) andavi	*you used to go, you were going (fam.)*
(Lei) andava	*you used to go, you were going (pol.)*
(lui) andava	*he used to go, he was going*
(lei) andava	*she used to go, she was going*
(noi) andavamo	*we used to go, we were going*
(voi) andavate	*you used to go, you were going (pl.)*
(loro) andavano (ahn-dáh-vah-noh)	*they used to go, they were going*

leggere (*to read*)

(io) leggevo	*I used to read, I was reading*
(tu) leggevi	*you used to read, you were reading (fam.)*
(Lei) leggeva	*you used to read, you were reading (pol.)*
(lui) leggeva	*he used to read, he was reading*
(lei) leggeva	*she used to read, she was reading*
(noi) leggevamo	*we used to read, we were reading*
(voi) leggevate	*you used to read, you were reading (pl.)*
(loro) leggevano (lej-jéh-vah-noh)	*they used to read, they were reading*

finire (*to finish*)

(io) finivo	*I used to finish, I was finishing*
(tu) finivi	*you used to finish, you were finishing (fam.)*
(Lei) finiva	*you used to finish, you were finishing (pol.)*
(lui) finiva	*he used to finish, he was finishing*
(lei) finiva	*she used to finish, she was finishing*
(noi) finivamo	*we used to finish, we were finishing*
(voi) finivate	*you used to finish, you were finishing (pl.)*
(loro) finivano (feeh-néeh-vah-noh)	*they used to finish, they were finishing*

EXERCISE
8·1

Translate the following sentences into Italian.

1. Giovanni, buy them! [them = *the boots*]

_____

2. Maria, don't take them! [them = *the croissants*]

_____

3. Mr. Mazzini, call me!

_____

4. Claudia, call me!

_____

5. Marco and Maria, speak to him!

_____

6. Let's finish it! [it = *the meat*]

_____

7. Mrs. Brunello, speak to us!

_____

Say that the given people used to do the following things awhile back, as indicated.

EXAMPLE: loro/andare/in montagna

Loro andavano in montagna.

8. io/leggere/molti libri

_____

9. tu/rimanere/sempre in casa

_____

10. mio fratello/credere/molte cose (*things*)

_____

11. mia sorella/uscire/spesso

_____

12. noi/venire/spesso/in Italia

_____

13. voi/vedere/mia cugina/spesso

_____

14. loro/capire/molto

_____

15. io/sapere/tante cose

_____

16. tu/non potere/mai uscire

_____

17. lui/finire/di lavorare/presto

_____

18. noi/dormire/fino a tardi

_____

Carry out the following conversation tasks.

19. Ask a friend if he/she likes to ski.

   _____

20. Ask a friend if he/she prefers swimming or tennis.

   _____

21. Say that there is a pool near here.

   _____

22. Say that you cannot go to the gym because the soccer championship is on TV.

   _____

23. Say that you'll go alone (by yourself).

   _____

24. Ask a friend if he/she likes basketball and car racing.

   _____

25. Ask a friend if he/she plays or engages in (*use* **praticare**) boxing, track and field, wrestling, or skating.

   _____

26. Say that you prefer to jog.

   _____

27. Say that you do not have a good partner.

   _____

Going out

Dialogo

The following is a typical conversation between friends planning to go out somewhere:

AMICO:	Non mi piace la musica classica!	*I don't like classical music!*
AMICA:	Dove vuoi uscire, allora?	*Where do you want to go out, then?*
AMICO:	Vorrei andare a ballare.	*I'd like to go dancing.*
AMICA:	Andiamo a un locale notturno?	*Shall we go to a nightclub?*
AMICO:	Forse no. Mi annoio sempre!	*Maybe not. I always get bored.*
AMICA:	Uffa! Sei impossibile!	*Ugh! You're impossible!*

NEW VOCABULARY

annoiarsi (annoiare + si)	to become bored	**locale notturno**	nightclub
ballare	to dance	**musica (móoh-zeeh-kah)**	music
classico (kláhs-seeh-koh)	classic		

Memory practice

Fill in the blanks with the appropriate words and expressions. Do this from memory, and then go back and check your answers.

Non mi piace la _____ classica!

Dove vuoi _____, allora?

Vorrei andare a _____.

Andiamo a un _____ notturno?

Forse no. Mi _____ sempre!

Uffa! Sei impossibile!

Language notes

There are very few irregular verbs in the imperfect. Of the verbs you have encountered so far, the main ones are conjugated for you:

essere (to be)

(io) ero	*I used to be, I was*
(tu) eri	*you used to be, you were* (fam.)
(Lei) era	*you used to be, you were* (pol.)
(lui) era	*he used to be, he was*
(lei) era	*she used to be, she was*
(noi) eravamo	*we used to be, we were*
(voi) eravate	*you used to be, you were* (pl.)
(loro) erano (éh-rah-noh)	*they used to be, they were*

dire (to say, to tell)

(io) dicevo	*I used to say, I was saying*
(tu) dicevi	*you used to say, you were saying* (fam.)
(Lei) diceva	*you used to say, you were saying* (pol.)
(lui) diceva	*he used to say, he was saying*
(lei) diceva	*she used to say, she was saying*
(noi) dicevamo	*we used to say, we were saying*
(voi) dicevate	*you used to say, you were saying* (pl.)
(loro) dicevano (deeh-chéh-vah-noh)	*they used to say, they were saying*

fare (to do, to make)

(io) facevo	*I used to do, I was doing*
(tu) facevi	*you used to do, you were doing* (fam.)
(Lei) faceva	*you used to do, you were doing* (pol.)
(lui) faceva	*he used to do, he was doing*
(lei) faceva	*she used to do, she was doing*
(noi) facevamo	*we used to do, we were doing*
(voi) facevate	*you used to do, you were doing* (pl.)
(loro) facevano (fah-chéh-vah-noh)	*they used to do, they were doing*

stare (*to stay*)

(io) stavo	*I used to stay, I was staying*
(tu) stavi	*you used to stay, you were staying (fam.)*
(Lei) stava	*you used to stay, you were staying (pol.)*
(lui) stava	*he used to stay, he was staying*
(lei) stava	*she used to stay, she was staying*
(noi) stavamo	*we used to stay, we were staying*
(voi) stavate	*you used to stay, you were staying (pl.)*
(loro) stavano (stáh-vah-noh)	*they used to stay, they were staying*

Dialogo

The previous conversation continues:

AMICA:	Vuoi andare a una discoteca?	*Would you like to go to a disco?*
AMICO:	Non mi piace la musica moderna.	*I don't like modern music.*
AMICA:	Allora andiamo al teatro.	*Then let's go to the theater.*
AMICO:	Assolutamente no!	*Absolutely not!*
AMICA:	Allora stiamo a casa a guardare la televisione.	*Then let's stay home and watch television.*

NEW VOCABULARY

assolutamente	absolutely	**moderno**	modern
assoluto	absolute	**teatro**	theater
discoteca	disco		

Memory practice

Fill in the blanks with the appropriate words and expressions. Do this from memory, and then go back and check your answers.

Vuoi andare a una _____?

Non mi piace la musica _____.

Allora andiamo al _____.

_____ no!

Allora stiamo a casa a guardare la _____.

Language notes

The progressive tenses are alternatives to the present and imperfect indicative. They simply allow you to zero in on an action, as in English: *I am trying, I was trying*, and so on. The tenses are made up of the verb **stare** plus the present participle. You already know how to conjugate **stare**, so all you need to know now is how to form the present participle.

To do so, drop the infinitive ending—**-are**, **-ere**, **-ire**—and add **-ando** for first-conjugation verbs and **-endo** for both second- and third-conjugation verbs.

andare	andando (*going*)
vedere	vedendo (*seeing*)
finire	finendo (*finishing*)

The present progressive is formed with **stare** in the present tense. Here is **andare** conjugated for you:

(io) sto andando	*I was going*
(tu) stai andando	*you were going* (fam.)
(Lei) sta andando	*you were going* (pol.)
(lui) sta andando	*he was going*
(lei) sta andando	*she was going*
(noi) stiamo andando	*we were going*
(voi) state andando	*you were going* (pl.)
(loro) stanno andando	*they were going*

The imperfect progressive is formed with **stare** in the imperfect. Here is **finire** conjugated fully for you:

(io) stavo finendo	*I was finishing*
(tu) stavi finendo	*you were finishing* (fam.)
(Lei) stava finendo	*you were finishing* (pol.)
(lui) stava finendo	*he was finishing*
(lei) stava finendo	*she was finishing*
(noi) stavamo finendo	*we were finishing*
(voi) stavate finendo	*you were finishing* (pl.)
(loro) stavano finendo	*they were finishing*

Note that the present participle of **dire** is **dicendo** and of **fare** it is **facendo**.

EXERCISE
8·2

Say that the person indicated was or used to do the following things, putting the italicized verb into the appropriate form of the imperfect tense. Note: there might be more than one verb in italics in a sentence.

EXAMPLE: tu/*essere*/sposato (-a)/quando ti ho conosciuto

Tu eri sposato (-a) quando ti ho conosciuto. (You were married when I met you.)

1. lui/*essere*/sposato/due anni fa/quando l'ho conosciuto

_____

2. Marco/*stare*/bene/ieri

_____

3. in Italia/*fare*/caldo/l'estate scorsa (*last summer*)

_____

4. io/*dire*/sempre la verità/quando/*essere*/bambino

_____

5. noi/*dire*/sempre la verità/quando/*essere*/bambini

_____

6. anche voi/*dire*/sempre la verità/quando/*essere*/bambini

_____

7. tu/*dire*/sempre tutto/a tua madre

_____

8. anche mia sorella/*dire*/sempre tutto/a sua madre

_____

9. loro/non/*dire*/mai/la verità/quando/*essere*/bambini

_____

10. io/non/*stare*/bene/ieri

_____

11. anche loro/non/*stare*/bene/ieri

_____

12. io/*fare*/molte cose (*things*)/quando/*essere*/bambino

_____

Replace the following verbs in the present indicative with the corresponding present progressive verbs.

EXAMPLE: Marco finisce la carne.

Marco sta finendo la carne.

13. Maria va in centro.

_____

14. Io leggo un bel romanzo.

_____

15. Tu dici la verità.

_____

16. Fa bel tempo.

_____

Now, replace the following verbs in the imperfect indicative with the corresponding imperfect progressive verbs.

EXAMPLE: Marco cercava il professore.

Marco stava cercando il professore.

17. Noi guardavamo la televisione ieri sera.

_____

18. Voi parlavate al professore.

_____

19. I miei amici uscivano quando hai chiamato.

_____

20. Io dormivo quando hai chiamato.

_____

Carry out the following conversation tasks.

21. Say that you like neither classical music nor modern music.

_____

22. Ask your partner where he/she wants to go out.

_____

23. Say that you would like to go dancing or to a nightclub.

_____

24. Say that you always get bored.

_____

25. Ask your partner if he/she wants to go to a disco.

_____

26. Ask him/her if he/she wants to go to the theater instead.

_____

27. Say that you prefer to stay home and watch television.

_____

Restaurants

Dialogo

The next conversation shows what one might say at a restaurant (**il ristorante**):

CAMERIERE: Cosa prendono?	_What would you like?_
AMICA: Per primo piatto, le lasagne.	_For my first dish, lasagne._
AMICO: Per me, invece, il minestrone.	_For me, instead, the minestrone._
AMICA: Ho cambiato idea. Prendo gli gnocchi.	_I changed my mind. I'll take the gnocchi._
CAMERIERE: E per secondo?	_And for second (main course)?_

AMICA:	Una cotoletta di vitello con contorno di patatine.	A veal cutlet with a side of fries.
AMICO:	E per me, la trota alla griglia, con un po' di verdure.	And for me, grilled trout with some vegetables.
CAMERIERE:	E da bere?	And to drink?
AMICA:	Una bottiglia di vino rosso e una bottiglia di acqua minerale.	A bottle of red wine and a bottle of mineral water.

NEW VOCABULARY

acqua minerale	mineral water	**idea**	idea
bere	to drink	**lasagne** (*f., pl.*)	lasagne
bottiglia	bottle	**minestrone** (*m.*)	minestrone
cambiare	to change	**patatina**	french fry
cameriere (-a)	waiter	**piatto**	plate, dish
contorno	side dish	**trota**	trout
cotoletta	cutlet	**vino**	wine
gnocco	dumpling	**vitello**	veal
griglia	grill		

Memory practice

Fill in the blanks with the appropriate words and expressions. Do this from memory, and then go back and check your answers.

Cosa _____?

Per primo piatto, le _____.

Per me, invece, il _____.

Ho cambiato idea. Prendo _____ gnocchi.

E per _____?

Una cotoletta di vitello con _____ di patatine.

E per me, la trota _____ griglia, con un po' di verdure.

E da _____?

Una bottiglia di vino rosso e una _____ di acqua minerale.

Language notes

Note the use of the polite **Loro** form used by the waiter: **Cosa prendono?** (*What are you having?*) The informal way of saying the same thing would be **Cosa prendete?** But this polite plural form is used commonly in very formal situations.

The words **primo** and **secondo** are ordinal numbers. The first ten are as follows:

1st	primo		4th	quarto
2nd	secondo		5th	quinto
3rd	terzo		6th	sesto

7th	settimo (séh-tteeh-moh)	9th	nono
8th	ottavo	10th	decimo (déh-cheeh-moh)

To construct the remaining ordinals, just drop the final vowel of the corresponding cardinal number and add **-esimo**.

11th	undic + esimo = undicesimo
24th	ventiquattr + esimo = ventiquattresimo

In the case of the numbers ending in **-tré**, take away the accent mark and add **-esimo**.

23rd	ventitré + esimo = ventitreesimo
33rd	trentatré + esimo = trentatreesimo

Ordinal numbers are adjectives, so they agree with the noun they modify.

il primo piatto (*the first dish*)	i primi piatti (*the first dishes*)
la seconda cosa (*the second thing*)	le seconde cose (*the second things*)

Note that *lasagne* in Italian is in the plural: **le lasagne**. And note that the article in front of **gn** in the masculine is **lo**, plural **gli**: **lo gnocco, gli gnocchi**.

The verb **bere** (*to drink*) is irregular in all the tenses we have covered so far. Here is a summary of its conjugations:

Present indicative

(io) bevo	*I drink*
(tu) bevi	*you drink* (fam.)
(Lei) beve	*you drink* (pol.)
(lui) beve	*he drinks*
(lei) beve	*she drinks*
(noi) beviamo	*we drink*
(voi) bevete	*you drink* (pl.)
(loro) bevono (béh-voh-noh)	*they drink*

Imperative

(tu) bevi	*drink* (fam.)
(Lei) beva	*drink* (pol.)
(noi) beviamo	*let's drink*
(voi) bevete	*drink* (fam., pl.)
(loro) bevano (béh-vah-noh)	*drink* (pol., pl.)

Imperfect

(io) bevevo	*I used to drink, I was drinking*
(tu) bevevi	*you used to drink, you were drinking (fam.)*
(Lei) beveva	*you used to drink, you were drinking (pol.)*
(lui) beveva	*he used to drink, he was drinking*
(lei) beveva	*she used to drink, she was drinking*
(noi) bevevamo	*we used to drink, we were drinking*
(voi) bevevate	*you used to drink, you were drinking (pl.)*
(loro) bevevano (beh-véh-vah-noh)	*they used to drink, they were drinking*

The past participle is **bevuto** and the verb is conjugated with **avere: ho bevuto, hai bevuto**, and so on. The present participle is **bevendo: sto bevendo, stavo bevendo**, and so on.

Here are some useful words related to the topic of this section:

il bicchiere	*the glass*	la forchetta	*the fork*
il coltello	*the knife*	la tazza	*the cup*
il cucchiaio	*the spoon*	il tovagliolo	*the napkin*

Dialogo

The restaurant scene continues:

CAMERIERE: Prendono il dessert o la frutta?	*Would you like dessert or fruit?*
AMICO: Cosa propone?	*What do you suggest?*
CAMERIERE: Abbiamo delle buonissime torte e anche del buon gelato.	*We have very good cakes and also some good ice cream.*
AMICO: Per me, un pezzo di torta al cioccolato.	*For me, a piece of chocolate cake.*
CAMERIERE: E per Lei?	*And for you?*
AMICA: Io vorrei mangiare un po' di frutta e un po' di formaggio.	*I would like to eat some fruit and some cheese.*
CAMERIERE: Prendono il caffè?	*Would you like some coffee?*
AMICA: Un espresso lungo.	*A long espresso.*
AMICO: E per me, un macchiato.	*And for me, a macchiato.*

NEW VOCABULARY

cioccolato	chocolate	**mangiare**	to eat
dessert (*m., inv.*)	dessert	**pezzo**	piece
gelato	ice cream	**proporre**	to propose
lungo	long	**torta**	cake
macchiato	with a dash of steamed milk		

Memory practice

Fill in the blanks with the appropriate words and expressions. Do this from memory, and then go back and check your answers.

Prendono il _____ o la frutta?

Cosa _____?

Abbiamo delle buonissime _____ e anche del buon _____.

Per me, un pezzo di torta _____ cioccolato.

E per Lei?

Io vorrei _____ un po' di frutta e un po' di formaggio.

Prendono il _____?

Un espresso _____.

E per me, un _____.

Language notes

Adverbs of manner are formed as follows.

◆ If the adjective ends in -**e** simply add -**mente** (the equivalent of -*ly* in English)

forte (*strong*)	fortemente (*strongly*)
felice (*happy*)	felicemente (*happily*)

◆ If, however, the ending is -**le** or -**re**, then the -**e** is dropped.

amichevole (*friendly*)	amichevolmente (*in a friendly manner*)
impossibile (*impossible*)	impossibilmente (*impossibly*)

◆ If the adjective ends in -**o**, change it to -**a** and add -**mente**.

sicuro (*sure*)	sicuramente (*surely*)
certo (*certain*)	certamente (*certainly*)

Here are some useful words to use in restaurants:

l'antipasto	*appetizer*	la mancia	*tip*
la cameriera	*waitress*	il menù (*inv.*)	*menu*
il cameriere	*waiter*	la prenotazione	*reservation*
il conto	*bill*		

EXERCISE
8·3

Write out the given ordinals in words, making sure that they agree with the noun.

EXAMPLE:　la *3rd* casa　　　　*terza*

1. il *4th* piatto　　　　_____

2. i *5th* anni　　　　_____

3. la *6th* casa　　　　_____

4. le *7th* volte   _____

5. l' *8th* piatto   _____

6. la *9th* volta   _____

7. la *10th* cosa   _____

8. il *45th* programma   _____

9. la *63rd* volta   _____

Give the appropriate present indicative form of **bere**.

EXAMPLE: Io non *bere* mai il caffè.   *bevo*

10. Anche tu non *bere* mai il caffè.   _____

11. Mio fratello *bere* sempre il latte.   _____

12. Anche noi *bere* spesso il latte.   _____

13. Ma voi non *bere* mai il latte.   _____

14. Anche loro non *bere* mai il caffè.   _____

Now, translate the following sentences into Italian.

15. I used to drink milk when I was a child.

_____

16. They also used to drink milk when they were children.

_____

17. Marco, drink all the water!

_____

18. They drank all the coffee already.

_____

Give the corresponding adverb of each adjective.

EXAMPLE: felice   *felicemente*

19. vivace   _____

20. assoluto   _____

21. preciso   _____

22. eccezionale   _____

Carry out the following conversation tasks.

23. As a waiter, ask two patrons politely what they will be having.

_____

24. Say that, for your first dish, you'll have lasagne, rather than minestrone.

_____

25. Say that you have changed your mind and will have gnocchi instead.

_____

26. Say that, for your second dish, you would like to eat a veal cutlet with a side of fries but that you cannot and, therefore, you will have grilled trout with a side of vegetables.

_____

27. Say that to drink you will have a bottle of white wine and a bottle of mineral water.

_____

28. Ask the waiter if you can have a spoon, a knife, and a fork.

_____

29. Now ask the waiter if you can have a new glass and a napkin.

_____

30. Ask where the cup is.

_____

31. Ask the waiter if you can have the menu.

_____

32. Say that you and your partner (_use the **noi** form of the verb_) do not have a reservation.

_____

33. Say that you do not want an appetizer.

_____

34. Ask the waiter (politely of course) if he/she can bring you the bill.

_____

35. Say that you do not have to leave (**lasciare**) a tip.

_____

36. Say that you would like some fruit and cheese.

_____

37. Say that you have changed your mind and prefer chocolate ice cream.

_____

38. Say that you want a long coffee, not a macchiato.

_____

·9· Traveling

Everybody loves to travel these days. Knowing how to carry out conversations at airports, train stations, and bus stations, not to mention at hotels, is a vital skill. This chapter will show you how to do so in Italian.

Trains and buses

Dialogo

The following conversation involves getting a train ticket:

PASSEGGERA:	Vorrei fare il biglietto per Firenze.	*I would like to purchase a ticket for Florence.*
BIGLIETTAIO:	Di andata e ritorno?	*Round-trip ticket?*
PASSEGGERA:	Sì.	*Yes.*
BIGLIETTAIO:	Quale classe?	*What class?*
PASSEGGERA:	La prima, per favore.	*First, please.*
BIGLIETTAIO:	Il treno partirà dal binario numero cinque.	*The train will be departing from track number five.*
PASSEGGERA:	Grazie.	*Thank you.*

NEW VOCABULARY

andata e ritorno	round-trip	**fare il biglietto**	to buy a (travel) ticket
bigliettaio (-a)	ticket agent	**partire (ess.)**	to leave, to depart
binario	track	**passeggero (-a)**	passenger
classe (*f.*)	class	**treno**	train

Memory practice

Fill in the blanks with the appropriate words and expressions. Do this from memory, and then go back and check your answers.

Vorrei _____ il biglietto per Firenze.

Di _____ e ritorno?

Sì.

Quale _____?

La prima, per favore.

Il treno _____ dal _____ numero
cinque.

Grazie.

Language notes

The verb form **partirà** is a future form. Let's start with first-conjugation, -are, verbs. To form the future, drop the -re, change the **a** to **e**, and add the following endings:

parlare (to speak)	
(io) parler**ò**	*I will speak*
(tu) parler**ai**	*you will speak* (fam.)
(Lei) parler**à**	*you will speak* (pol.)
(lui) parler**à**	*he will speak*
(lei) parler**à**	*she will speak*
(noi) parler**emo**	*we will speak*
(voi) parler**ete**	*you will speak* (pl.)
(loro) parler**anno**	*they will speak*

Note that if the verb ends in **-ciare** or **-giare**, the ending is changed to **-cer** and **-ger**, respectively.

(io) comin**cer**ò	*I will begin*
(loro) man**ger**anno	*they will eat*

If it ends in **-care** or **-gare**, as in **pagare** (*to pay*), then an **h** is added to indicate that the hard sound is to be retained.

(tu) cer**ch**erai	*you will look for*
(loro) pa**gh**eranno	*they will pay*

Here is some useful vocabulary related to the theme of this section:

arrivare	*to arrive*	la partenza	*departure*
l'arrivo	*arrival*	il posto	*seat*
l'orario	*schedule, timetable*	la stazione	*station*

Dialogo

Here's the kind of conversation you might hear at a bus depot:

PASSEGGERO:	Scusi, l'autobus per Firenze è in orario?	*Excuse me, is the bus for Florence on time?*
BIGLIETTAIO:	È in anticipo di qualche minuto.	*It's early by a few minutes.*
PASSEGGERO:	Ho ancora tempo. C'è un'edicola qui vicino?	*I still have some time. Is there a newsstand nearby?*
BIGLIETTAIO:	È alla fermata.	*It's at the bus stop.*
PASSEGGERO:	Grazie.	*Thank you.*

autobus (*m., inv.*)	bus	**in orario**	on time
edicola (eh-déeh-koh-lah)	newsstand	**minuto**	minute
fermata	stop	**tempo**	time
in anticipo (ahn-téeh-cheeh-poh)	early		

Memory practice

Fill in the blanks with the appropriate words and expressions. Do this from memory, and then go back and check your answers.

Scusi, l'autobus per Firenze è in _____?

È in _____ di qualche minuto.

Ho ancora tempo. C'è un'_____ qui vicino?

È alla _____.

Grazie.

Language notes

To form the future of second- and third-conjugation verbs, just drop the **-re** and add the same endings as those required for first-conjugation verbs.

leggere (*to read*)	
(io) legger**ò**	*I will read*
(tu) legger**ai**	*you will read* (fam.)
(Lei) legger**à**	*you will read* (pol.)
(lui) legger**à**	*he will read*
(lei) legger**à**	*she will read*
(noi) legger**emo**	*we will read*
(voi) legger**ete**	*you will read* (pl.)
(loro) legger**anno**	*they will read*

finire (*to finish*)	
(io) finir**ò**	*I will finish*
(tu) finir**ai**	*you will finish* (fam.)
(Lei) finir**à**	*you will finish* (pol.)
(lui) finir**à**	*he will finish*
(lei) finir**à**	*she will finish*
(noi) finir**emo**	*we will finish*
(voi) finir**ete**	*you will finish* (pl.)
(loro) finir**anno**	*they will finish*

Put each italicized verb into the future tense.

1. Maria *arrivare* domani. _____

2. Noi *parlare* solo italiano in Italia. _____

3. Noi *pagare* il conto. _____

4. Voi non *mangiare* la carne. _____

5. Io *cominciare* a mangiare presto. _____

6. Anche tu *cercare* un posto in prima. _____

7. Tu *chiedere* un posto in prima, vero? _____

8. Io *credere* tutto quello che mi dici. _____

9. Noi *prendere* il treno delle sedici. _____

10. Domani *piovere* molto. _____

11. Loro *leggere* quel nuovo romanzo. _____

12. Io *capire* tutto quello che mi dici. _____

13. Loro *finire* alle diciassette. _____

14. Noi *partire* domani per Torino. _____

15. Voi *dormire* fino a tardi, vero? _____

16. Mio fratello *uscire* con Bruna stasera. _____

Carry out the following conversation tasks.

17. Say that you would like to purchase a round-trip ticket to Rome.

_____

18. Say that you would like a first-class ticket.

_____

19. Say that the train will be departing from track number 12.

_____

20. Say that you will arrive at the station on time.

_____

21. Say that your friend will arrive early by a few minutes.

_____

22. Say that bus departure is at 2 p.m. and that arrival is at 5 p.m. (*Use official time.*)

_____

23. Say that you still have some time.

_____

24. Ask if there is a newsstand nearby.

_____

Accommodations

Dialogo

The next conversation takes place at a hotel check-in counter:

IMPIEGATA: Scusi, ha fatto la prenotazione?	*Excuse me, did you make a reservation?*
TURISTA: Sì, per una camera che dà sulla Piazza della Signoria.	*Yes, for a room that looks onto Piazza della Signoria.*
IMPIEGATA: Vediamo! Abbiamo una camera singola.	*Let' see! We have a single room.*
TURISTA: Va bene! A quanto viene?	*That's fine! How much does it come to?*
IMPIEGATA: A quattrocento dollari americani a notte.	*Four hundred American dollars a night.*
TURISTA: La prendo.	*I'll take it.*

NEW VOCABULARY			
dare	to give	**dollaro (dóh-lah-roh)**	dollar
dare su	to look onto	**singolo (séehn-goh-loh)**	single

Memory practice

Fill in the blanks with the appropriate words and expressions. Do this from memory, and then go back and check your answers.

Scusi, ha fatto la _____?

Sì, per una camera che _____ su Piazza della Signoria.

Vediamo! Abbiamo una camera _____.

Va bene! A quanto _____?

A quattrocento _____ americani a notte.

La prendo.

Language notes

The form **dà** is from the verb **dare** (*to give*), which is irregular throughout the conjugations. It is a very useful verb to know. Here are the conjugations of **dare** in the tenses covered so far in this book:

Present indicative

(io) do	*I give*
(tu) dai	*you give* (fam.)
(Lei) dà	*you give* (pol.)
(lui) dà	*he gives*
(lei) dà	*she gives*
(noi) diamo	*we give*
(voi) date	*you give* (pl.)
(loro) danno	*they give*

Imperative

(tu) da'	*give* (fam.)
(Lei) dia	*give* (pol.)
(noi) diamo	*let's give*
(voi) date	*give* (fam., pl.)
(loro) diano (déeh-ah-noh)	*give* (pol., pl.)

Imperfect

(io) davo	*I used to give, I was giving*
(tu) davi	*you used to give, you were giving* (fam.)
(Lei) dava	*you used to give, you were giving* (pol.)
(lui) dava	*he used to give, he was giving*
(lei) dava	*she used to give, she was giving*
(noi) davamo	*we used to give, we were giving*
(voi) davate	*you used to give, you were giving* (pl.)
(loro) davano (dáh-vah-noh)	*they used to give, they were giving*

Future

(io) darò	*I will give*
(tu) darai	*you will give* (fam.)
(Lei) darà	*you will give* (pol.)
(lui) darà	*he will give*
(lei) darà	*she will give*
(noi) daremo	*we will give*
(voi) darete	*you will give* (pl.)
(loro) daranno	*they will give*

The past participle is **dato**, and the verb is conjugated with **avere: ho dato**, **hai dato**, and so on. The present participle is **dando: sto dando**, **stavo dando**, and so on.

Needless to say, there are verbs that have irregular forms in the future. Of the verbs you have come across so far, the following are the most useful to know. Note that you do not need to memorize them all. Just look at how they are formed, and you will see a pattern in most, namely, that you drop two vowels from the infinitive. They are conjugated here as a kind of reference section for you:

andare (to go)

(io) and**rò**	*I will go*
(tu) and**rai**	*you will go* (fam.)
(Lei) and**rà**	*you will go* (pol.)
(lui) and**rà**	*he will go*
(lei) and**rà**	*she will go*
(noi) and**remo**	*we will go*
(voi) and**rete**	*you will go* (pl.)
(loro) and**ranno**	*they will go*

avere (to have)

(io) av**rò**	*I will have*
(tu) av**rai**	*you will have* (fam.)
(Lei) av**rà**	*you will have* (pol.)
(lui) av**rà**	*he will have*
(lei) av**rà**	*she will have*
(noi) av**remo**	*we will have*
(voi) av**rete**	*you will have* (pl.)
(loro) av**ranno**	*they will have*

bere (to drink)

(io) ber**rò**	*I will have*
(tu) ber**rai**	*you will have* (fam.)
(Lei) ber**rà**	*you will have* (pol.)
(lui) ber**rà**	*he will have*
(lei) ber**rà**	*she will have*
(noi) ber**remo**	*we will have*
(voi) ber**rete**	*you will have* (pl.)
(loro) ber**ranno**	*they will have*

dire (to say)

(io) di**rò**	*I will say*
(tu) di**rai**	*you will say* (fam.)
(Lei) di**rà**	*you will say* (pol.)
(lui) di**rà**	*he will say*
(lei) di**rà**	*she will say*
(noi) di**remo**	*we will say*
(voi) di**rete**	*you will say* (pl.)
(loro) di**ranno**	*they will say*

dovere (to have to)

(io) dov**rò**	*I will have to*
(tu) dov**rai**	*you will have to* (fam.)
(Lei) dov**rà**	*you will have to* (pol.)
(lui) dov**rà**	*he will have to*
(lei) dov**rà**	*she will have to*
(noi) dov**remo**	*we will have to*
(voi) dov**rete**	*you will have to* (pl.)
(loro) dov**ranno**	*they will have to*

essere (to be)

(io) sa**rò**	*I will be*
(tu) sa**rai**	*you will be* (fam.)
(Lei) sa**rà**	*you will be* (pol.)
(lui) sa**rà**	*he will be*
(lei) sa**rà**	*she will be*
(noi) sa**remo**	*we will be*
(voi) sa**rete**	*you will be* (pl.)
(loro) sa**ranno**	*they will be*

fare (to do, to make)

(io) fa**rò**	*I will do*
(tu) fa**rai**	*you will do* (fam.)
(Lei) fa**rà**	*you will do* (pol.)
(lui) fa**rà**	*he will do*
(lei) fa**rà**	*she will do*
(noi) fa**remo**	*we will do*
(voi) fa**rete**	*you will do* (pl.)
(loro) fa**ranno**	*they will do*

potere (to be able to)

(io) pot**rò**	*I will be able to*
(tu) pot**rai**	*you will be able to* (fam.)
(Lei) pot**rà**	*you will be able to* (pol.)
(lui) pot**rà**	*he will be able to*
(lei) pot**rà**	*she will be able to*
(noi) pot**remo**	*we will be able to*
(voi) pot**rete**	*you will be able to* (pl.)
(loro) pot**ranno**	*they will be able to*

sapere (to know)

(io) sap**rò**	*I will know*
(tu) sap**rai**	*you will know* (fam.)

(Lei) saprà	*you will know (pol.)*
(lui) saprà	*he will know*
(lei) saprà	*she will know*
(noi) sapremo	*we will know*
(voi) saprete	*you will know (pl.)*
(loro) sapranno	*they will know*

venire (*to go*)

(io) verrò	*I will go*
(tu) verrai	*you will go (fam.)*
(Lei) verrà	*you will go (pol.)*
(lui) verrà	*he will go*
(lei) verrà	*she will go*
(noi) verremo	*we will go*
(voi) verrete	*you will go (pl.)*
(loro) verranno	*they will go*

volere (*to want*)

(io) vorrò	*I will want*
(tu) vorrai	*you will want (fam.)*
(Lei) vorrà	*you will want (pol.)*
(lui) vorrà	*he will want*
(lei) vorrà	*she will want*
(noi) vorremo	*we will want*
(voi) vorrete	*you will want (pl.)*
(loro) vorranno	*they will want*

Here is some useful vocabulary related to the theme of this section:

l'ascensore	*elevator*	l'ingresso	*entrance*
l'atrio	*lobby*	il piano	*floor*
la chiave	*key*	l'uscita	*exit*

Dialogo

The following conversation shows how one might complain about poor hotel service:

TURISTA: Non tornerò mai più in quest'albergo!	*I'll never come back to this hotel!*
IMPIEGATA: Perché?	*Why?*
TURISTA: La colazione non è buona e le camere sono sporche!	*The breakfast is not good, and the rooms are dirty!*
IMPIEGATA: Non capisco!	*I don't understand!*
TURISTA: E l'ascensore non funziona quasi mai!	*And the elevator almost never works!*
IMPIEGATA: Si calmi, signore! Le faremo uno sconto.	*Stay calm, sir! We will work out a discount for you.*

albergo	hotel	**quasi**	almost
calmarsi	to stay calm	**sconto**	discount
colazione (*f.*)	breakfast	**sporco**	dirty
funzionare	to work (function)		

Memory practice

Fill in the blanks with the appropriate words and expressions. Do this from memory, and then go back and check your answers.

Non _____ mai più in quest'albergo!

Perché?

La _____ non è buona e le camere sono _____!

Non capisco!

E l'_____ non funziona quasi mai!

Si calmi, signore! Le faremo uno _____.

Language notes

You have come across the form **vorrei** often in this book. It is a conditional tense form. The conditional is formed exactly like the future. The only difference is the set of endings. So, drop the **-re** of all three conjugations, changing the **a** of the first-conjugation verbs to **e**, just as you do with the future tense, then add these endings instead of the future endings:

parlare (*to speak*)

(io) parler**ei**	*I would speak*
(tu) parler**esti**	*you would speak* (fam.)
(Lei) parler**ebbe**	*you would speak* (pol.)
(lui) parler**ebbe**	*he would speak*
(lei) parler**ebbe**	*she would speak*
(noi) parler**emmo**	*we would speak*
(voi) parler**este**	*you would speak* (pl.)
(loro) parler**ebbero**	*they would speak*

leggere (*to read*)

(io) legger**ei**	*I would read*
(tu) legger**esti**	*you would read* (fam.)
(Lei) legger**ebbe**	*you would read* (pol.)
(lui) legger**ebbe**	*he would read*
(lei) legger**ebbe**	*she would read*
(noi) legger**emmo**	*we would read*
(voi) legger**este**	*you would read* (pl.)
(loro) legger**ebbero**	*they would read*

finire (*to finish*)

(io) fini**rei**	*I would finish*
(tu) fini**resti**	*you would finish* (fam.)
(Lei) fini**rebbe**	*you would finish* (pol.)
(lui) fini**rebbe**	*he would finish*
(lei) fini**rebbe**	*she would finish*
(noi) fini**remmo**	*we would finish*
(voi) fini**reste**	*you would finish* (pl.)
(loro) fini**rebbero**	*they would finish*

The same verbs that are irregular in the future are also irregular in the conditional. Here are a few examples:

FUTURE	CONDITIONAL
io avrò (*I will have*)	io avrei (*I would have*)
tu sarai (*you will be*)	tu saresti (*you would be*)
lui andrà (*he will go*)	lui andrebbe (*he would go*)
noi vorremo (*we will like*)	noi vorremmo (*we would like*)
voi saprete (*you will know*)	voi sapreste (*you would know*)
loro verranno (*they will come*)	loro verrebbero (*they would come*)

EXERCISE 9·2

Give the present indicative forms of **dare** *as indicated.*

1. Noi *dare* questo al professore. _____

2. Anch'io *dare* qualcosa al professore. _____

3. Anche tu gli *dare* qualcosa? _____

4. Mia sorella *dare* molte cose alle amiche. _____

5. Anche voi *dare* molte cose agli amici. _____

6. Loro non ci *dare* mai niente. _____

Translate the following sentences into Italian.

7. I gave those shoes to my brother.

_____

8. You used to give your sister many things.

_____

9. He will give me some money to go out tonight.

_____

10. They would give me some money, but they can't.

_____

Give the corresponding conditional form for each future form.

FUTURE	CONDITIONAL
11. lui mangerà	_____
12. io cercherò	_____
13. noi partiremo	_____
14. tu verrai	_____
15. voi saprete	_____
16. io pagherò	_____
17. tu sarai	_____
18. lei avrà	_____
19. io vorrò	_____
20. loro diranno	_____
21. io farò	_____

Carry out the following conversation tasks.

22. Say that you have not made a reservation.

_____

23. Say that you would like a room that looks onto the square (**la piazza**).

_____

24. Say that you would like a single room, not a double room (**camera doppia**).

_____

25. Ask how much it comes to per night.

_____

26. Ask if you could have two keys.

_____

27. Say that the elevator doesn't work.

_____

28. Ask if you could have a room on the sixth floor.

_____

29. Ask where the lobby is.

_____

30. Say that the exit is here.

_____

31. Ask where the hotel entrance is.

_____

32. Say that you will never come back to this hotel.

_____

33. Say that the breakfast is almost never good.

_____

34. Say that your room is dirty.

_____

35. Say that you would like a discount.

_____

At the airport

Dialogo

The next conversation typifies what one might say at an airport check-in counter:

IMPIEGATO:	Il Suo biglietto, per favore.	*Your ticket, please.*
PASSEGGERO:	Eccolo!	*Here it is!*
IMPIEGATO:	Il volo partirà tra mezz'ora.	*The flight is leaving in half an hour.*
PASSEGGERO:	Meno male!	*Thank goodness!*
IMPIEGATO:	Ecco la Sua carta d'imbarco!	*Here's your boarding pass!*
PASSEGGERO:	Dov'è l'uscita?	*Where's the gate?*
IMPIEGATO:	Laggiù, davanti a quel segnale.	*Down there, in front of that sign.*

NEW VOCABULARY

carta d'imbarco	boarding pass		**tra**	within
laggiù	down there		**uscita**	gate, exit
Meno male!	Thank goodness!		**volo**	flight
segnale (*m.*)	sign			

Memory practice

Fill in the blanks with the appropriate words and expressions. Do this from memory, and then go back and check your answers.

Il Suo _____, per favore.

Eccolo!

Il _____ partirà _____ mezz'ora.

Meno _____!

Ecco la Sua _____ d'imbarco!

Dov'è l'_____?

_____, davanti a quel segnale.

Language notes

Note that pronouns are attached to **ecco**.

Ecco**lo**.	*Here **it** is/Here **he** is.*
Ecco**mi**.	*Here **I** am.*

The preposition **tra** can also be written and pronounced as **fra**. And it also means *between*. Here is some useful vocabulary related to the theme of this section:

il bagaglio	*baggage*	un posto al finestrino	*window seat*
il posto	*seat*	la valigia	*suitcase*
un posto al corridoio	*aisle seat*		

Dialogo

Here's the type of announcement that is usually given at takeoff:

ASSISTENTE: Signore e signori, siete pregati di allacciare la cintura di sicurezza. Il decollo è previsto tra qualche minuto. A decollo compiuto, serviremo il pasto. Il comandante e l'intero equipaggio, vi augurano un buon viaggio!

Ladies and gentleman, please (you are asked) fasten your seat belts. Takeoff is expected in a few minutes. After takeoff, we will serve the meal. The captain and the entire crew wish you a good trip!

NEW VOCABULARY

allacciare	to fasten	**essere pregato**	to be asked
augurare	to wish	**essere previsto**	to be expected
cintura di sicurezza	seat belt	**intero**	entire
comandante (*m./f.*)	captain	**pasto**	meal
compiuto	completed	**servire**	to serve
decollo	takeoff	**viaggio**	trip
equipaggio	crew		

Memory practice

Fill in the blanks with the appropriate words and expressions. Do this from memory, and then go back and check your answers.

Signore e signori, siete _____ di allacciare la _____ di sicurezza. Il _____ è previsto tra qualche minuto. A decollo _____, serviremo il pasto. Il _____ e l'intero _____, vi augurano un _____ viaggio!

Language notes

In previous chapters you have come across three particles: **ne, ci, si**. All three come before the verb. **Ne** usually replaces a partitive phrase. Note that in compound tenses the past participle agrees with **ne**.

Vuoi **dei piselli**?	*Would you like **some peas**?*
Sì, **ne** voglio.	*Yes, I would like **some**.*
Quanti **libri** hai comprato?	*How many **books** did you buy?*
Ne ho comprati due.	*I bought **two** (**of them**).*
Hai **delle mele**?	*Do you have **some apples**?*
No, non **ne** ho.	*No, I do not have **any**.*

Ci means *there* and is an alternative to **lì** and other place adverbs.

Quando vai **in centro**?	*When are you going **downtown**?*
Ci vado domani.	*I am going (**there**) tomorrow.*

Si is used to mean the impersonal *one*. Note that the verb is singular or plural according to what the sentence is about.

Si compra quel vestito in centro.	***One buys** that dress downtown.*
Si comprano quegli stivali in centro.	***One buys** those dresses downtown.*

EXERCISE
9·3

Replace the italicized phrases with an appropriate pronoun, and then rewrite the entire sentence, making all necessary changes.

EXAMPLE: Ecco *le vostre carte d'imbarco.*

Eccole. (Here they are.)

1. Ecco *il Suo biglietto.*

_____

2. Ecco *i vostri bagagli.*

_____

3. Ecco *le mie valige.*

_____

4. Ecco *la Sua valigia.*

_____

*Now replace the italicized phrase with **ne**, **ci**, or **si** as the case may be, and then rewrite the entire sentence, making all necessary changes.*

5. Prendo *delle pere.*

_____

6. Ho mangiato *dei fagioli.*

_____

7. Vado *in l'Italia* domani.

_____

8. Andrò *in centro* nel pomeriggio.

_____

9. *Uno* (personal "one") deve dire sempre la verità.

_____

10. *Uno* (personal "one") compra quelle cose in centro.

_____

Carry out the following conversation tasks.

11. Give your ticket to the agent pointing it out. (*Here is my ticket*)

_____

12. Say that the flight will be departing in half an hour.

_____

13. Say "Thank heavens!"

_____

14. Say "Here's your boarding pass."

_____

15. Ask where the gate is.

_____

16. Say that it's down there in front of that sign.

_____

17. Say that you would like a window seat, not an aisle seat.

_____

18. Pretend you are a flight attendant and inform the passengers to fasten their seat belt.

_____

19. Say that takeoff is expected in a few minutes.

_____

20. Say that the captain and the entire crew wish the passengers a good trip.

_____

This and that

In the previous nine chapters, we covered the main areas of everyday conversation. In this chapter, we will deal with a few others, including how to talk about cars, the activities related to driving, how to express your emotions, and a few other common conversational topics.

Driving

Dialogo

The following conversation is a typical one when renting a car:

IMPIEGATO:	Che tipo di macchina vorrebbe noleggiare?	*What kind of car would you like to rent?*
AUTISTA:	Una piccola.	*A small one.*
IMPIEGATO:	Posso vedere la Sua patente e la Sua carta di credito?	*May I have your driver's license and your credit card?*
AUTISTA:	Certo. Qual è il prezzo?	*Of course. What's the price?*
IMPIEGATO:	Solo centocinquanta euro al giorno.	*Only one hundred fifty euro per day.*
AUTISTA:	Allora la prendo per una settimana.	*Then I'll take it for a week.*
IMPIEGATO:	Firmi qui. Ecco le chiavi.	*Sign here. Here are the keys.*

NEW VOCABULARY
---

autista (*m./f.*)	driver	**noleggiare**	to rent
carta di credito (kréh-deeh-toh)	credit card	**patente** (*f.*)	driver's license
giorno	day	**prezzo**	price
macchina (máh-keeh-nah)	car	**tipo**	type

Memory practice

Fill in the blanks with the appropriate words and expressions. Do this from memory, and then go back and check your answers.

Che tipo di macchina vorrebbe _____?

Una piccola.

Posso vedere la Sua _____ e la Sua carta di _____?

Certo. Qual è il _____?

Solo centocinquanta euro al _____.

Allora la prendo per una settimana.

_____ qui. Ecco le chiavi.

Language notes

Reflexive verbs are conjugated just like regular verbs. You can recognize a reflexive infinitive because it has an -**si** (*oneself*) at the end.

lavare (*to wash*)	lavarsi (*to wash oneself*)
mettere (*to put*)	mettersi (*to put on, to wear*)
divertire (*to entertain*)	divertirsi (*to enjoy oneself*)

To conjugate reflexive verbs in the present, imperfect, future, and conditional, just conjugate them in the usual fashion, placing the reflexive pronouns, **mi**, **ti**, **si**, **ci**, **vi**, **si**, before the verb in the sentence. Thus, conjugate **lavarsi** as you would **lavare**, **mettersi** as you would **mettere**, and **divertirsi** as you would **divertire**. So, a form such as **si divertono** is translated as *they enjoy themselves*. That's all there is to it.

For convenience, here are these three verbs conjugated for you in the mentioned tenses:

lavarsi	mettersi	divertirsi
Present indicative		
(io) **mi** lavo	(io) **mi** metto	(io) **mi** diverto
(tu) **ti** lavi	(tu) **ti** metti	(tu) **ti** diverti
(Lei) **si** lava	(Lei) **si** mette	(Lei) **si** diverte
(lui) **si** lava	(lui) **si** mette	(lui) **si** diverte
(lei) **si** lava	(lei) **si** mette	(lei) **si** diverte
(noi) **ci** laviamo	(noi) **ci** mettiamo	(noi) **ci** divertiamo
(voi) **vi** lavate	(voi) **vi** mettete	(voi) **vi** divertite
(loro) **si** lavano	(loro) **si** mettono	(loro) **si** divertono

lavarsi	mettersi	divertirsi
Imperfect		
(io) **mi** lavavo	(io) **mi** mettevo	(io) **mi** divertivo
(tu) **ti** lavavi	(tu) **ti** mettevi	(tu) **ti** divertivi
(Lei) **si** lavava	(Lei) **si** metteva	(Lei) **si** divertiva
(lui) **si** lavava	(lui) **si** metteva	(lui) **si** divertiva
(lei) **si** lavava	(lei) **si** metteva	(lei) **si** divertiva
(noi) **ci** lavavamo	(noi) **ci** mettevamo	(noi) **ci** divertivamo
(voi) **vi** lavavate	(voi) **vi** mettevate	(voi) **vi** divertivate
(loro) **si** lavavano	(loro) **si** mettevano	(loro) **si** divertivano

Future

(io) **mi** laverò	(io) **mi** metterò	(io) **mi** divertirò
(tu) **ti** laverai	(tu) **ti** metterai	(tu) **ti** divertirai
(Lei) **si** laverà	(Lei) **si** metterà	(Lei) **si** divertirà
(lui) **si** laverà	(lui) **si** metterà	(lui) **si** divertirà
(lei) **si** laverà	(lei) **si** metterà	(lei) **si** divertirà
(noi) **ci** laveremo	(noi) **ci** metteremo	(noi) **ci** divertiremo
(voi) **vi** laverete	(voi) **vi** metterete	(voi) **vi** divertirete
(loro) **si** laveranno	(loro) **si** metteranno	(loro) **si** divertiranno

Conditional

(io) **mi** laverei	(io) **mi** metterei	(io) **mi** divertirei
(tu) **ti** laveresti	(tu) **ti** metteresti	(tu) **ti** divertiresti
(Lei) **si** laverebbe	(Lei) **si** metterebbe	(Lei) **si** divertirebbe
(lui) **si** laverebbe	(lui) **si** metterebbe	(lui) **si** divertirebbe
(lei) **si** laverebbe	(lei) **si** metterebbe	(lei) **si** divertirebbe
(noi) **ci** laveremmo	(noi) **ci** metteremmo	(noi) **ci** divertiremmo
(voi) **vi** lavereste	(voi) **vi** mettereste	(voi) **vi** divertireste
(loro) **si** laverebbero	(loro) **si** metterebbero	(loro) **si** divertirebbero

Previously, you have come across the following reflexive verbs:

annoiarsi	*to become bored*
calmarsi	*to stay calm*
chiamarsi	*to call oneself, to be named*
provarsi	*to try on*

Here is some useful vocabulary related to the theme of this section:

l'acceleratore	*the gas pedal*	il freno	*the brake*
il clacson	*the horn*	lo sportello	*the door*
il faro	*the headlight*	il volante	*the steering wheel*
il finestrino	*the passenger window*		

Also note that **noleggiare** means *to rent something*. Renting an apartment, on the other hand, is **affittare**. Note also that *to sell* is **vendere** (véhn-deh-reh).

Dialogo

The next conversation might take place at a service station (**stazione di servizio**):

Autista:	Il pieno, per favore.	*Fill it up, please.*
Benzinaio:	Normale o super?	*Regular or super?*
Autista:	Normale.	*Regular.*
Benzinaio:	Dopo, vuole controllare l'olio?	*After, would you like to check the oil?*
Autista:	No, ma pulisca il parabrezza.	*No, but clean the windshield.*
Benzinaio:	C'è abbastanza aria nelle gomme?	*Is there enough air in the tires?*
Autista:	Sì, credo.	*Yes, I believe.*

abbastanza	enough	**normale**	normal
aria	air	**parabrezza** (*m.*)	windshield
controllare	to check, to control	**pieno**	full
dopo	after	**pulire**	to clean
gomma	tire		

Memory practice

Fill in the blanks with the appropriate words and expressions. Do this from memory, and then go back and check your answers.

Il _____, per favore.

_____ o super?

Normale.

_____, vuole controllare l'olio?

No, ma _____ il parabrezza.

C'è _____ aria nelle gomme?

Sì, credo.

Language notes

In the present perfect (and all other compound tenses), all reflexive verbs are conjugated with **essere**. Here are the previous three verbs fully conjugated for you. Note that the past participle of **mettere** is **messo**.

lavarsi	mettersi	divertirsi
(io) **mi** sono lavato (-a)	(io) **mi** sono messo (-a)	(io) **mi** sono divertito (-a)
(tu) **ti** sei lavato (-a)	(tu) **ti** sei messo (-a)	(tu) **ti** sei divertito (-a)
(Lei) **si** è lavato (-a)	(Lei) **si** è messo (-a)	(Lei) **si** è divertito (-a)
(lui) **si** è lavato	(lui) **si** è messo	(lui) **si** è divertito
(lei) **si** è lavata	(lei) **si** è messa	(lei) **si** è divertita
(noi) **ci** siamo lavati (-e)	(noi) **ci** siamo messi (-e)	(noi) **ci** siamo divertiti (-e)
(voi) **vi** siete lavati (-e)	(voi) **vi** siete messi (-e)	(voi) **vi** siete divertiti (-e)
(loro) **si** sono lavati (-e)	(loro) **si** sono messi (-e)	(loro) **si** sono divertiti (-e)

Say that the indicated people are doing the following things, using the present indicative of the verbs.

EXAMPLE: (io) am putting on a sweater.

Io mi metto una maglia.

1. (tu) are washing yourself at (in) this moment.

   _____

2. (lui) is putting on a new jacket.

   _____

3. (lei) is enjoying herself at the movies.

   _____

4. (noi) are getting bored downtown.

   _____

5. (voi) are trying on various types of shoes.

   _____

6. (loro) are enjoying themselves in Italy.

   _____

Now say that the same people were doing or used to do the same things, using the imperfect indicative of the verbs.

EXAMPLE: (io) was putting on a sweater.

Io mi mettevo una maglia.

7. (tu) were washing yourself yesterday.

   _____

8. (lui) was putting on a new jacket.

   _____

9. (lei) used to enjoy herself at the movies.

   _____

10. (noi) were getting bored downtown.

    _____

11. (voi) were trying on various types of shoes.

    _____

12. (loro) used to enjoy themselves in Italy.

    _____

Now, say that the same people did do the same things, using the present perfect of the verbs.

EXAMPLE: (**io**) put on a sweater.

Io mi sono messo (-a) una maglia.

13. (**tu**) washed yourself yesterday.

_____

14. (**lui**) put on a new jacket.

_____

15. (**lei**) enjoyed herself at the movies.

_____

16. (**noi**) got bored downtown.

_____

17. (**voi**) tried on various types of shoes.

_____

18. (**loro**) enjoyed themselves in Italy.

_____

Finally, say that the same people would and will (in fact) do the same things, using both the conditional and future tenses of the verbs.

EXAMPLE: (**io**) would and in fact will put on a sweater.

Io mi metterei e infatti (in fact) mi metterò una maglia.

19. (**tu**) would and in fact will wash yourself today.

_____

20. (**lui**) would and in fact will put on a new jacket.

_____

21. (**lei**) would and in fact will enjoy herself at the movies.

_____

22. (**noi**) would and in fact will get bored downtown.

_____

23. (**voi**) would and in fact will try on various types of shoes.

_____

24. (**loro**) would and in fact will enjoy themselves in Italy.

_____

Carry out the following conversation tasks.

25. Ask someone (politely) what type of car he/she would like to rent.

    _____

26. Ask someone (politely) if you can see his/her driver's license and credit card.

    _____

27. Ask what the price is.

    _____

28. Say that the price is only one hundred euros per day.

    _____

29. Ask someone politely to sign here.

    _____

30. Say that the brakes are not working.

    _____

31. Say that the steering wheel, the gas pedal, the headlights, and the horn are new.

    _____

32. Say that the doors and windows are very modern.

    _____

33. Ask a gas attendant to fill up your car.

    _____

34. Say that, after, you should (**dovrei**) check the oil and the air in the tires, and clean the windshield.

    _____

Being emotional

Dialogo

If you need to express your emotions in Italian, the following conversation shows how you might do so:

AMICO:	Hai finito di studiare?	*Did you finish studying?*
AMICA:	Macché! Sono stufa! Voglio uscire!	*No way! I'm so fed up! I want to go out!*
AMICO:	Dai, devi studiare un po' di più e poi usciamo.	*Come on, you have to study a bit more, and then we'll go out!*
AMICA:	Non ce la faccio più!	*I can't take it any longer!*
AMICO:	Calmati! Vedrai che domani starai meglio.	*Calm down! Tomorrow, you'll see, you'll feel better.*

essere stufo	to be fed up	**Macché!**	No way!
farcela (fare + ci + la)	to be able to take it	**studiare**	to study

Memory practice

Fill in the blanks with the appropriate words and expressions. Do this from memory, and then go back and check your answers.

Hai finito di _____?

Macché! Sono _____! Voglio uscire!

_____, devi studiare un po' di più e poi usciamo.

Non ce la _____ più!

_____! Vedrai che domani starai meglio.

Language notes

The form **calmati** is in the imperative. In fact, on familiar forms of reflexive verbs, you attach the reflexive pronoun to the end (as you did object pronouns).

Tu forms

Marco, calmati!	*Marco, calm yourself!*
Maria, divertiti!	*Maria, enjoy yourself!*

Noi forms

Calmiamoci!	*Let's calm down!*
Divertiamoci!	*Let's enjoy ourselves!*

Voi forms

Marco e Maria, mettetevi cose nuove!	*Marco and Maria, put on new things!*
Ragazzi, divertitevi!	*Guys, enjoy yourselves!*

Recall that in the negative imperative, the **tu**-form is the infinitive of the verb. To add on the pronoun, drop the -**e** of the infinitive.

Marco, non metterti quell'abito!	*Marco, don't put on that suit!*
Maria, non provarti quella giacca!	*Maria, don't try on that jacket!*

Recall that when you add on the pronoun, you retain the word stress of the verb as it was before the add-on.

With the polite forms (**Lei, Loro**), however, the pronoun goes before.

Lei forms

Signor Rossini, si calmi!	*Mr. Rossini, calm yourself!*
Signorina, si diverta!	*Miss, enjoy yourself!*

Loro forms

Signore e signori, si calmino!	*Ladies and gentlemen, calm yourselves!*

Dialogo

The "emotional chatter" continues:

Amico:	Mi ami, bella?	*Do you love me, my beautiful one?*
Amica:	Con tutto il cuore. Sei il mio vero amore!	*With all my heart. You're my true love!*
Amico:	Anche tu sei tutto per me.	*You, too, mean everything to me.*
Amica:	Ti voglio un mondo di bene!	*I care the world for you!*
Amico:	Ah, sono veramente fortunato!	*Ah, I am really lucky!*

NEW VOCABULARY

cuore (*m.*)	heart	**mondo**	world
fortunato	fortunate, lucky	**volere bene a**	to care for, to love

---

Memory practice

Fill in the blanks with the appropriate words and expressions. Do this from memory, and then go back and check your answers.

Mi ami, bella? _____

Con tutto il cuore. Sei il mio vero amore! _____

Anche tu sei tutto per me. _____

Ti voglio un mondo di bene! _____

Ah, sono veramente fortunato! _____

Language notes

Throughout this book you have been using simple forms of **piacere**. Actually, the verb means, literally, *to be pleasing to*. If you keep this in mind, you'll be able to use it all the time. Note that it is irregular in the present indicative.

(io) piaccio a	*I am pleasing to*
(tu) piaci a	*you are pleasing to* (fam.)
(Lei) piace a	*you are pleasing to* (pol.)
(lui) piace a	*he is pleasing to*
(lei) piace a	*she is pleasing to*
(noi) piacciamo a	*we are pleasing to*
(voi) piacete a	*you are pleasing to* (pl.)
(loro) piacciono a	*they are pleasing to*

Using a verb like **piacere** means using indirect object pronouns often. Here are some examples:

Mi piace la torta.

I like the cake	=	*The cake is pleasing to me.*

Gli piacciono le mele.

He likes the apples	=	*The apples are pleasing to him.*

Io piaccio a Maria.

Maria likes me.   =   *I am pleasing to Maria.*

Note that in the present perfect, **piacere** is conjugated with **essere**.

Mi è piaciut**a** la torta.

I liked the cake   =   *The cake was pleasing to me.*

Gli sono piaciut**e** le mele.

He liked the apples   =   *The apples were pleasing to him.*

Io sono piaciut**o** (-**a**) a Maria.

Maria liked me.   =   *I was pleasing to Maria.*

EXERCISE
10·2

Tell the following people to do the indicated things.

1. Tell Marco to calm down.

   _____

2. Tell Maria to not be bored.

   _____

3. Tell Mr. Verdi to put on a tie.

   _____

4. Tell Mrs. Marchi to try on these boots.

   _____

5. Tell Bruna to enjoy herself with your brother.

   _____

Now translate the following sentences into Italian.

6. I like french fries.

   _____

7. Maria likes my brother.

   _____

8. We like him.

   _____

9. I used to like french fries many years ago.

   _____

10. Maria will like your brother.

    _____

11. We did not like him.

_____

Carry out the following conversation tasks.

12. Ask a friend if he/she has finished studying.

_____

13. Say "No way!" and that you're fed up with studying.

_____

14. Say that you can't take it any longer.

_____

15. Tell your friend that you love him/her with all your heart.

_____

16. Tell him/her that he/she is your true love.

_____

17. Say that you care the world for him/her.

_____

18. Say that you are very fortunate.

_____

Reporting and gossiping

Dialogo

Gossip, unfortunately, is also part of everyday life, as the next conversation illustrates:

AMICO:	Hai sentito quello che ha fatto Antonio?	*Did you hear what Antonio did?*
AMICA:	Mi hanno detto che si è divorziato!	*They told me he got divorced!*
AMICO:	No, ma sta andando con un'altra donna.	*No, but he is going with another woman.*
AMICA:	Mascalzone!	*Rascal!*
AMICO:	E sua moglie è così brava. Povera donna!	*And his wife is so nice. Poor woman!*

NEW VOCABULARY

divorziarsi	to get divorced	**sentire**	to hear
mascalzone	rascal, scoundrel		

Memory practice

Fill in the blanks with the appropriate words and expressions. Do this from memory, and then go back and check your answers.

Hai _____ quello che ha fatto Antonio?

Mi hanno detto che si è _____!

No, ma sta _____ con un'altra donna.

Mascalzone!

E sua moglie è _____ brava. Povera donna!

Language notes

As you have discovered in previous chapters, to compare things in terms of *more* simply use **più**.

Maria è intelligente.	Mia sorella è **più** intelligente.
Maria is intelligent.	*My sister is **more** intelligent.*
Marcello è alto.	Alessandro è **più** alto.
Marcello is tall.	*Alessandro is tall**er**.*

To use comparisons in terms of *less*, use **meno**.

Maria è intelligente.	La mia amica è **meno** intelligente.
Maria is intelligent	*My friend is **less** intelligent.*
Marcello è alto.	Alessandro è **meno** alto.
Marcello is tall.	*Alessandro is **less** tall.*

Dialogo

The gossip continues:

AMICO:	Che cosa ti ha detto Maria ieri?	*What did Maria tell you yesterday?*
AMICA:	Mi ha detto che ha comprato un iPod.	*She told me she bought an iPod.*
AMICO:	A me, invece, ha detto che non aveva denaro.	*She told me, instead, that she had no money.*
AMICA:	Lei dice troppe bugie!	*She tells too many lies!*
AMICO:	Come molta gente.	*Like many people.*

NEW VOCABULARY

bugia   lie   **gente** (*f.*)   people

Memory practice

Fill in the blanks with the appropriate words and expressions. Do this from memory, and then go back and check your answers.

Che cosa ti ha _____ Maria ieri?

Mi ha detto che ha _____ un iPod.

A me, invece, ha detto che non _____ denaro.

Lei dice troppe _____!

Come molta _____.

Language notes

In comparisons, use **di** when comparing different subjects.

Mia sorella è più intelligente **di** Maria.	*My sister is more intelligent **than** Maria.*
Mio fratello è più alto **del** suo amico.	*My brother is taller **than** his friend.*
Io sono meno simpatico **della** mia amica.	*I am less nice **than** my friend.*

Use **che** if comparing the same subject.

Mia sorella è più intelligente **che** simpatica.	*My sister is more intelligent **than** (she is) nice.*
Mio fratello è più sincero **che** timido.	*My brother is more sincere **than** (he is) shy.*
Io sono meno simpatico **che** intelligente.	*I am less nice **than** (I am) intelligent.*

EXERCISE 10·3

Say that the indicated person(s) is/are more or less than the other person(s). Follow the example.

EXAMPLE: Marco è alto./Alessandro/*more*

Alessandro è più alto di Marco.

1. Maria è brava./Sara/*more*

   _____

2. Quell'uomo è simpatico./quella donna/*less*

   _____

3. Il professore è intelligente./la dottoressa/*more*

   _____

4. Quegli studenti sono sinceri./i nostri amici/*more*

   _____

Now, say that the indicated person(s) has more of the second characteristic. Follow the example.

EXAMPLE: Marco è alto./grande

Marco è più grande che alto.

5. Maria è brava./amichevole

   _____

6. Quell'uomo è simpatico./generoso

_____

7. Il professore è intelligente./vivace

_____

8. Quegli studenti sono sinceri./timido

_____

Carry out the following conversation tasks.

9. Ask a friend if he/she has heard what Antonio has done.

_____

10. Say that someone told you that he got divorced.

_____

11. Say that he is going with another woman.

_____

12. Call him a rascal.

_____

13. Say that his poor wife is so nice.

_____

14. Say that Maria told you that she did not have any money.

_____

15. Say that she tells too many lies.

_____

16. Say "Like many people."

_____

Overall review

To see how much you recall about conversing in Italian, carry out the following conversation tasks. Note that these follow the order of the themes in the book and reflect material contained in the various dialogues.

1. Greet Miss Marchi in the morning.

   _____

2. Greet Giovanni and ask him how he is.

   _____

3. Say that your name is Marco Signori.

   _____

4. Say, informally, that it is a pleasure to know someone.

   _____

5. Ask, politely, if someone can help you.

   _____

6. Say that you like that novel very much.

   _____

7. Say that you would like an espresso coffee, please.

   _____

8. Ask how much they cost.

   _____

9. Using official time, say that it is two twenty (in the afternoon).

   _____

10. Ask at what time the program is ending.

    _____

11. Ask a friend how old he/she is.

    _____

12. Say that you were born in 1995.

_____

13. Say that you live on 46 National Street.

_____

14. Say that you live in Perugia, right downtown.

_____

15. Ask someone, politely, if he/she can tell you were Boccaccio Street is.

_____

16. Tell someone (politely) that he/she has to go left, not right.

_____

17. Answer the phone saying hello and asking who it is.

_____

18. Tell a friend that he/she has to send you a text message with his/her cell phone.

_____

19. Say that you do not like blond men.

_____

20. Tell your friend: "Look what a beautiful woman!"

_____

21. Say that your brother is charming and intelligent.

_____

22. Say that your (female) friend is very nice.

_____

23. Say that Alessandro is just like his father.

_____

24. Say that he is very cute.

_____

25. Say that you have a toothache, asking a friend if he/she knows a good dentist.

_____

26. Say that you do not want to be a teacher.

_____

27. Say that you are looking for a job in someone's company.

_____

28. Ask someone what his/her marital status is.

_____

29. Say that this house is very small.

_____

30. Say that you need to buy new furniture.

_____

31. Say that you would also like some peas and some fresh beans.

_____

32. Say that you would also like some very good cheese.

_____

33. As a clothing clerk, ask a customer (politely, of course) if he/she wants to try on this brown jacket.

_____

34. Ask how much these boots cost.

_____

35. Say that you would like to deposit this money into your account.

_____

36. Say that you would like to exchange these bills for smaller change (coins).

_____

37. Say that yesterday it was really too cold.

_____

38. Say that tomorrow you would like to go downtown.

_____

39. Say that your brother went out with Bruna.

_____

40. Say that in autumn the leaves fall.

_____

41. Say that you love the Christmas holidays.

_____

42. Say that you prefer those shoes. Thus, you will take them.

_____

43. Tell Marco not to go downtown because it is raining.

_____

44. Say that when you were a child, you used to go often to the movies.

_____

45. Tell the waiter that for your first dish you prefer minestrone.

_____

46. Say that the train is departing from track number 6.

_____

47. Say that the breakfast is never good in this hotel.

_____

48. Say that takeoff is expected in a few minutes.

_____

49. Say that you would like to rent a small car.

_____

50. Say that he is a rascal and that he is going with another woman.

_____

Glossary

A

a at, to
a casa mia at my house
a che ora at what time
a destra to the right
a domani see you tomorrow
a presto see you soon
a sinistra to the left
abbastanza enough
abitare to live, to dwell
abito suit
acceleratore (*m.*) gas pedal
acqua water
acqua minerale mineral water
adesso now
affittare to rent an apartment, house, etc.
agosto August
albergo hotel
alla moda in style, fashionable
allacciare to fasten
allora then, thus
alto tall
altro anything else, other
amare to love
americano American
amichevole friendly
amico (-a) friend
amore (*m.*) love
anche (anche io *or* anch'io) also, too
ancora still, yet
andare (ess.) to go
andata e ritorno round-trip
anello ring
anno year
annoiarsi to become bored
antipasto appetizer
appuntamento appointment, date
aprile April
arancione (*inv.*) orange
architetto architect
aria air
arrivare (ess.) to arrive
arrivederci good-bye (*informal*)

arrivederLa good-bye (*formal*)
arrivo arrival
ascensore (*m.*) elevator
aspettare to wait for
assai quite, rather
assoluto absolute
atletica leggera track and field
atrio lobby
attraversare to cross
augurare to wish
autista (*m./f.*) driver
autobus (*m., inv.*) bus
automobilismo car racing
autunno autumn, fall
avere to have
avere bisogno di to need (to have need of)
avere fame to be hungry
avere ragione to be right
avere voglia di to feel like
avere... anni to be ... old
avventura adventure
avvocato lawyer
azzurro blue

B

bagaglio baggage
bagno bathroom
ballare to dance
bambino (-a) little boy/girl, child
banca bank
bancomat (*m.*) automatic teller
bar coffee place, bar
barbiere (*m.*) barber
barista (*m./f.*) bartender
basso short
bastare (ess.) to be enough
bello beautiful
bene well
bere to drink
bianco white
bicchiere glass
bigliettaio (-a) ticket agent
biglietto bill, ticket

binario track
biondo blond
blu (*inv.*) dark blue
borsa purse
bottiglia bottle
bravo good
bruno dark-haired
brutto ugly
bugia lie
Buon compleanno! Happy birthday!
buon pomeriggio good afternoon
buona notte good night
buonasera good evening
buongiorno good morning, good day, hello
buono good

C

cadere (ess.) to fall
caffè coffee
calcio soccer
caldo hot, warm
calmarsi to stay calm
cambiare to change, to exchange
camera bedroom
cameriere (-a) waiter
camerino change room
camicetta blouse
camicia shirt
campionato championship, playoffs
capire (-isc) to understand
carino cute
carne (f.) meat
caro dear
carta d'imbarco boarding pass
carta di credito credit card
casa house
cellulare cell phone
centro downtown, center of town
cercare to search for, to look for
certo certainly, of course
che what, that, who, which
Che ore sono?/Che ora è? What time is it?
chi who
chiamare to call
chiamarsi to call oneself, to be named
chiave (f.) key
chiedere to ask for
chiesa church
chilo kilogram
ci vediamo See you
cinema (m., inv.) cinema, movies
cintura belt
cintura di sicurezza seat belt
cioccolato chocolate
circa around, nearly
clacson (m., inv.) car horn
classe (f.) class

classico classic
cliente (m./f.) customer
colazione (f.) breakfast
coltello knife
comandante (m./f.) captain
come how, like
Come si chiama? (pol.) What is your name?
Come stai? (fam.)/sta? (pol.) How are you?
Come ti chiami? (fam.) What's your name?
Come va? How's it going?
cominciare to begin, to start
commemorativo commemorative
commesso (-a) clerk
compiuto completed
compleanno birthday
comprare to buy
con with
condominio condo
consiglio advice
contento happy, content
conto account, bill
contorno side dish
controllare to check, to control
convenire (ess.) to be better to
cornetto croissant
cosa thing
così so, thus
costare (ess.) to cost
cotoletta cutlet
cravatta tie
creare to create
credere to believe
crescere (ess.) to grow
cucchiaio spoon
cucina kitchen
cugino (-a) cousin
cuore (m.) heart

D

d'accordo fine, I agree
da from (for)
da leggere to read
da portare via to take out
dare to give
dare su to look onto
davanti in front
decollo takeoff
denaro money
dentista (m./f.) dentist
depositare to deposit
desiderare to desire, to want
dessert (m., inv.) dessert
devo andare I have to go
di of
di nuovo again
dicembre December
dimenticare to forget

dire to tell, to say
diritto straight ahead
discoteca disco
dispositivo device
ditta company (business)
divano sofa
diventare (ess.) to become
diverso diverse, various, several
divertire to entertain
divertirsi to enjoy oneself
divorziarsi to get divorced
dollaro dollar
domanda question
domani tomorrow
domenica Sunday
donna woman
dopo after
dormire to sleep
dottore (*m.*) Dr./doctor
dottoressa (*f.*) Dr./doctor
dove where
dovere to have to, must
dozzina dozen

E

e and
eccezionale exceptional
ecco here is
edicola newsstand
educato well-mannered
elettricista (*m./f.*) electrician
equipaggio crew
esperienza experience
espresso espresso
esserci to be there
essere (ess.) to be
essere innamorato to be/fall in love
essere nato (-a) to be born
essere pregato to be asked
essere previsto to be expected
essere sposato (-a) to be married
estate (*f.*) summer
euro euro

F

fa ago
fagiolo bean
famiglia family
farcela to be able to take/manage it
fare to do, to make
fare il biglietto to buy a (travel) ticket
fare il footing to jog
faro car headlight
fastidioso fussy
febbraio February
felice happy
festa feast, holiday, party

fetta slice
figlia daughter
figlio son
finestrino passenger window
finire (-isc) to finish
firmare to sign
foglia leaf
forchetta fork
formaggio cheese
forse maybe
forte strong, hard
fortunato fortunate, lucky
fra between, within
fragola strawberry
francobollo stamp
fratello brother
freddo cold
freno brake
fresco fresh
frigorifero refrigerator
frutta fruit
funzionare to work (function)

G

garage (*m.*) garage
gelato ice cream
generi alimentari groceries
generoso generous
gennaio January
gente (*f.*) people
già already
giacca jacket
giallo yellow
giorno day
giovedì Thursday
girare to turn
giro tour
giugno June
gnocco dumpling
gomma tire
gonna skirt
grande big
grazie thank you
grigio gray
griglia grill
guardare to look at, to watch
guida guide

I

idea idea
ieri yesterday
impiegato (-a) office worker
impossibile impossible
in in
in anticipo early
in ferie on vacation
in orario on time

in punto on the dot
in saldo on sale
indirizzo address
informatica computer, informatics
ingresso entrance
insegnante (*m./f.*) teacher
insieme together
intelligente intelligent
intero entire
intervista interview
invece instead
inverno winter
io I
isolato block
italiano Italian

L

laggiù down there, over there
lasagne (*f., pl.*) lasagne
latte (*m.*) milk
laurea degree
lavare to wash
lavarsi to wash oneself
lavorare to work
lavoro work, job
leggere to read
Lei you (*pol.*)
letto bed
lì there
libro book
lieto delighted
locale notturno nightclub
lotta wrestling
luglio July
lunedì Monday
lungo long

M

ma but
Macché! No way!
macchiato with a dash of steamed milk
macchina car
madre mother
maggio May
maglia sweater
magnifico magnificent
mai ever
mal di denti toothache
mamma mom
mancia tip (gratuity)
mandare to send
mangiare to eat
mare (*m.*) sea
marito husband
marrone (*inv.*) brown
martedì Tuesday
marzo March

mascalzone (*m.*) rascal, scoundrel
matematica mathematics
mattina morning
meccanico mechanic
medico medical doctor
meglio better
mela apple
meno less
Meno male! Thank goodness!
menù (*m., inv.*) menu
mercato market
mercoledì Wednesday
messaggino text, message
mettere to put
mettersi to put on, to wear
mezzanotte (*f.*) midnight
mezzo half
mezzogiorno noon
mi chiamo my name is
mi presento let me introduce myself
Mi può aiutare? (*pol.*) Can you help me?
Mi puoi aiutare? (*fam.*) Can you help me?
minestrone (*m.*) minestrone
minuto minute
mobile (*m.*) piece of furniture
mobile mobile
moderno modern
modulo form
moglie wife
molto very, much, a lot
momento moment
mondo world
montagna mountain(s)
musica music

N

Natale (*m.*) Christmas
natalizio of Christmas
né neither, nor
neanche neither
negozio store
nero black
nessuno no one
neve (*f.*) snow
nevicare to snow
niente nothing
no no
noioso boring, fussy
noleggiare to rent a vehicle, a movie, etc.
non not
non c'è problema no problem
non importa it doesn't matter
nonna grandmother
nonno grandfather
normale normal
nostro our
notte (*f.*) night

novembre November
nulla nothing
numero number
nuoto swimming
nuovo new

O

o or
occhio eye
odiare to hate
oggi today
ogni each, every
ora hour, time
orario schedule, timetable
ottimista optimistic
ottimo excellent
ottobre October

P

padre father
pagare to pay
palestra gym
pallacanestro basketball
pane (*m.*) bread
panino bun sandwich
pantaloni (*m., pl.*) pants
papà (*m., inv.*) dad
parabrezza (*m.*) windshield
parlare to speak
partenza departure
partire (**ess.**) to leave, to depart
Pasqua Easter
passeggero (**-a**) passenger
pasto meal
patatina french fry
patente (*f.*) driver's license
pattinaggio skating
per for, through
per favore please
pera pear
perché why, because
però however
pesca peach
pesce (*m.*) fish
pezzo piece
piacere (**ess.**) to like, to be pleasing to, a pleasure
Piacere di conoscerti. A pleasure to know you.
Piacere di fare la Sua (*pol.*) **conoscenza.** A pleasure to make your acquaintance.
piano floor
pianta plant
piatto plate, dish
piazza city square
piccolo little, small
pieno full
piovere to rain
piscina swimming pool

pisello pea
più more
piuttosto rather
pizzicheria delicatessen
poi then
poltrona armchair
pomeriggio afternoon
portare to wear
posto seat
posto al corridoio aisle seat
posto al finestrino window seat
potere to be able to, can
pratico practical
preciso precise (precisely)
preferire (**-isc**) to prefer
prego you're welcome
prelevare to withdraw
prendere to take
prenotazione (*f.*) reservation
presentare to present, to introduce
prestare to lend
presto soon, early
prezzo price
primavera spring
professore (*m.*) professor
professoressa (*f.*) professor
programma (*m.*) program
Pronto! Hello!
proporre to propose
proprio just, right, really
prosciutto prosciutto ham
prossimo next
provare to try
provarsi to try on
pugilato boxing
pulire to clean
purtroppo unfortunately

Q

qualche some
qualcosa something
qualcuno someone
quale which, what
quando when
quanto how much
quasi almost
quello che that which, whatever
qui here

R

ragazzo (**-a**) boy (girl), youth
ricordare to remember
rimanere (**ess.**) to remain
ristorante (*m.*) restaurant
romantico romantic
romanzo novel
rosso red

S

sabato Saturday
sala da pranzo dining room
salame (*m.*) salami
salotto living room
sapere to know
sbagliare to make a mistake
sbocciare to blossom
scarpa shoe
sciare to ski
sconto discount
scuola school
scusi excuse me (*pol.*)
se if
secondo according to, second, main course
segnale (*m.*) sign
semaforo traffic lights
sembrare (**ess.**) to seem
sempre always
sentire to hear, to feel
senz'altro without doubt, likely
senza without
sera evening
serie series
servire to serve
settembre September
settimana week
sì yes
sicuro sure
signora Mrs., madam, lady
signore Mr., sir, gentleman
signorina Miss, Ms.
simpatico nice, charming
sincero sincere
singolo single
SMS (*m.*) text message
soldi money
sole (*m.*) sun
solo only, alone
sorella sister
spesa food shopping
spesso often
spicciolo coin, small change
sporco dirty
sportello door
stare (**ess.**) to stay, to be
stare bene a to look good on
stasera tonight
stato civile marital status
stazione station
stazione (*f.*) **di servizio** service station
stesso same
stivale boot
strada road, street
studente (*m.*) male student
studentessa (*f.*) female student
studiare to study

stufo fed up
stupido stupid
su on
subito right away
supermercato supermarket

T

taglia size
tanto many, a lot
tardi late
tavolo table
tazza cup
teatro theater
telefonare to phone
televisione (*f.*) television
tempo weather, time
tennis (*m., inv.*) tennis
terribile terrible
timido shy, timid
tipo type
tirare vento to be windy
tornare (**ess.**) to return, to come back
torta cake
tovagliolo napkin
tra within
treno train
troppo too, too much
trota trout
trovare to find
tuo your (*fam.*)
turista (*m./f.*) tourist (*male or female*)
tutti everyone
tutti e due both
tutto everything
TV (*f.*) TV

U

ufficiale official
un po' a bit
università (*f.*) university
uomo man
uscire (**ess.**) to go out
uscita exit, gate

V

va bene OK
vacanza vacation
valigia suitcase
vedere to see
vendere to sell
venerdì Friday
venire (**ess.**) to come
vento wind
verde green
verdura vegetables
verità (*f.*) truth
vero true, right

vestito dress
vetrina store window
via street
viaggio trip
vicino near
vigile (*m.*) traffic policeman
vino wine
viola (*inv.*) purple
vitello veal
vivace lively, vivacious

volante (*m.*) steering wheel
volere to want
volere bene a to care for, to love
volo flight
volta time (occurrence)
vorrei I would like

Z

zia aunt
zio uncle

Answer key

1 Making contact

1·1   1. uomo   2. Mr. Verdi   3. sì   4. Professor Marchi   5. A presto   6. Dr. Bruni   7. e
8. Professor Santucci   9. Lei   10. Mrs. (Ms.) Marchi   11. donna   12. Dr. Santucci
13. certo   14. how   15. domani   16. thank you   17. tu   18. very   19. bene
20. Buongiorno.   21. Buon pomeriggio.   22. A domani.   23. ArrivederLa.
24. Arrivederci./Ciao.   25. Come va?   26. Ciao.   27. Buongiorno, signora Verdi.
28. Buonasera, signor Marchi.   29. Buon pomeriggio, professoressa Santucci.   30. Ciao,
Marcello.   31. Buonanotte.

1·2   1. Molto lieto.   2. Piacere di fare la Sua conoscenza.   3. italiana   4. americano
5. sono   6. sei   7. è   8. Come si chiama?   9. Come ti chiami?   10. Piacere di
conoscerti.   11. (Io) sono italiano (-a).   12. Devo andare.

1·3   1. Che (cosa) è?   2. Chi è?   3. Dov'è (Dove è) il commesso?   4. Perché non mi puoi
aiutare?   5. isolati   6. libri   7. italiani   8. romanzi   9. uomini   10. dottori
11. professori   12. ho   13. hai   14. ha   15. abbiamo   16. avete   17. hanno
18. Mi piace il nuovo romanzo.   19. Mi piacciono i libri.   20. Mi piace il dottore.
21. Mi piacciono i professori.   22. Ho bisogno di un nuovo libro da leggere.   23. Le
piacciono i romanzi d'avventura?   24. Il libro è in vetrina.   25. Ecco un romanzo
d'avventura.   26. Va bene.   27. Scusi, mi può aiutare?   28. Scusa, mi puoi aiutare?
29. Via Nazionale è qui a sinistra, non a destra.   30. Certo, signorina.   31. È a due
isolati.   32. Non c'è problema.   33. Maria non è americana.   34. È italiana, Maria?/
Maria è italiana?

2 Numbers, time, dates

2·1   1. i francobolli   2. i cornetti   3. i libri   4. i panini   5. i romanzi   6. una casa
7. una nuova casa/una casa nuova   8. una donna bella   9. due euro   10. tre panini
11. quattro romanzi   12. cinque cornetti   13. sei espressi/sei caffè espressi   14. sette
uomini   15. otto libri belli   16. nove euro   17. dieci francobolli commemorativi
18. tredici uomini belli   19. quattordici donne belle   20. quindici case belle   21. sedici,
diciassette, diciotto   22. diciannove, trentotto   23. duecento cinquantatré   24. novecento
sessantadue   25. duemila ottanta   26. Vorrei un caffè espresso, per favore.   27. Altro?
28. Vorrei due o tre cornetti subito.   29. Ho molta fame.   30. Va bene, vorrei comprare
due panini da portare via.   31. C'è una festa a casa mia stasera.   32. Prego.   33. C'è un
nuovo bar/un bar nuovo in via Nazionale.   34. Non ci sono nuovi libri/libri nuovi in
vetrina.   35. Ecco un espresso.   36. Quanto costano i francobolli?   37. Ogni panino
costa undici euro.   38. Allora, ne prendo solo dodici.

2·2   1. È l'una e dieci del pomeriggio./Sono le tredici e dieci.   2. Sono le tre e trenta/mezzo del
pomeriggio./Sono le quindici e trenta.   3. Sono le quattro e dodici del pomeriggio./Sono
le sedici e dodici.   4. Sono le nove e dieci della mattina.   5. Sono le dieci e quindici/un
quarto della mattina.   6. Sono le sette e trentacinque della sera./Sono le diciannove e
trentacinque.   7. Sono le nove e quarantotto della sera./Sono le ventuno e quarantotto.
8. È mezzogiorno.   9. È mezzanotte.   10. Tu torni alle diciannove e quindici/un quarto.
11. La donna comincia alle otto e trentotto.   12. Noi cominciamo alle dieci e trenta/mezzo.

13. Voi tornate alle ventidue e venti.   14. Loro cominciano alle undici e dieci.   15. Io comincio alle tredici e cinque.   16. Che ora è?/Che ore sono?   17. No, non è tardi.   18. (Io) ho un appuntamento alle quattro precise del pomeriggio/alle sedici precise col professore.   19. Maria torna alle otto in punto della sera/alle venti in punto.   20. Quando finisce?   21. Finisce alle dieci della sera/alle venti circa.   22. Il giro comincia troppo tardi.   23. C'è un giro che comincia a mezzogiorno?   24. Allora, (io) torno domani alla stessa ora.

2·3   1. Oggi è lunedì, il primo gennaio.   2. Oggi è martedì, l'otto febbraio.   3. Oggi è mercoledì, il dieci marzo.   4. Oggi è giovedì, il dodici aprile.   5. Oggi è venerdì, il ventotto maggio.   6. Oggi è sabato, il ventitré giugno.   7. Oggi è domenica, il quattro luglio.   8. Quanti   9. Quanti   10. Quanto   11. Quante   12. Alessandro è nato nel 1994.   13. La moglie è nata nel 1987.   14. Il marito è nato nel 1984.   15. Quanti ne abbiamo (oggi)?   16. Se non sbaglio, è il compleanno di Maria.   17. Buon compleanno!   18. Quanti anni hai?   19. Quanti anni ha?   20. (Io) ho trentasei anni.   21. (Tu) sembri ancora un bambino.   22. Che giorno è?   23. È terribile!   24. Il marito dimentica sempre tutto.   25. Ma anche noi dimentichiamo sempre tutto.   26. Ricordo in che anno è nato (-a).

3   Getting information

3·1   1. americani   2. appuntamenti   3. avventure   4. bambini   5. bambine   6. dottoresse   7. romanzi   8. sere   9. mogli   10. dottori   11. Come sta tuo fratello?   12. Come state (voi)?   13. Come sta (Lei)?   14. Come stanno i bambini?   15. (io) vengo, so, conosco   16. (tu) vieni, sai, conosci   17. (lui/lei) viene, sa, conosce   18. (noi) veniamo, sappiamo, conosciamo   19. (voi) venite, sapete, conoscete   20. (loro) vengono, sanno, conoscono   21. Dove abiti adesso?   22. Dove abita adesso, signora Marchi?   23. (Io) abito a Firenze.   24. La signora Marchi abita in Italia.   25. Il signor Verdi abita in via Dante.   26. (Io) abito vicino a Maria.   27. (Io) abito negli Stati Uniti.   28. Qualcuno ha detto che (io) sono sposato (-a).   29. Per adesso, mi piace la libertà.   30. Il romanzo che leggo è nuovo.   31. Come sta tuo fratello?   32. È sposato e ha bambini.   33. Non sono sicuro (-a) quando verrà la prossima volta.   34. (Lui) viene spesso a Roma.   35. (Io) so leggere in italiano.   36. (Io) non conosco il professore d'italiano.

3·2   1. devi, vai, dici, fai, puoi   2. deve, va, dice, fa, può   3. dobbiamo, andiamo, diciamo, facciamo, possiamo   4. dovete, andate, dite, fate, potete   5. devono, vanno, dicono, fanno, possono   6. devo, vado, dico, faccio, posso   7. un semaforo   8. una strada   9. uno studente   10. una studentessa   11. uno zio   12. una zia   13. i bambini belli   14. la donna bella   15. i vigili alti   16. la madre alta   17. le case grandi   18. il bambino grande   19. (Scusi), mi sa dire dov'è via Dante?   20. Vada a destra per un isolato e poi giri a sinistra al semaforo.   21. Devo attraversare la strada?   22. Vada diritto per ancora tre isolati.   23. Lì c'è via Macchiavelli?/C'è via Macchiavelli lì?   24. Ecco il/un bancomat.   25. Come si fa per andarci?   26. Vada a nord per un po'.   27. È vicino alla chiesa.   28. È proprio davanti alla chiesa.   29. Non può sbagliare.   30. Vada a sud e poi a est per un po'.

3·3   1. i bambini   2. la strada   3. gli studenti   4. l'avventura   5. gli anni   6. l'euro   7. i caffè (*Recall that nouns ending in an accented vowel do not change.*)   8. l'uomo   9. voglio   10. vogliono   11. vuoi   12. vuole   13. vogliamo   14. volete   15. Giovanni, ti chiamo stasera col (mio) cellulare.   16. È meglio mandarmi un SMS/un messaggino.   17. Non ho un dispositivo mobile.   18. Pronto!   19. Chi parla?   20. Sono io.   21. Laura, che vuoi?   22. Signora Verdi, che vuole?   23. Non c'è.   24. Non importa.   25. Chiamo/Telefono più tardi.

4   People

4·1   1. questo uomo sicuro   2. quello studente stupido   3. questi commessi bassi   4. quegli uomini belli   5. questo signore stupido   6. quell'americano grande   7. quegli italiani bassi   8. questa donna brutta   9. queste bambine timide   10. quella casa piccola   11. quelle case brutte   12. quell'americana bassa   13. quelle americane alte   14. al semaforo   15. dai commessi   16. dello zio   17. nell'occhio   18. sul SMS   19. alle donne   20. nella strada   21. dei bambini   22. degli uomini   23. Guarda che uomo bello!   24. Guarda che donna bella!   25. L'uomo è troppo alto per me.   26. Mi piacciono gli uomini biondi con gli occhi blu.   27. Non mi piacciono gli uomini bruni che sono troppo alti.   28. Non sembra intelligente, ma sembra molto simpatico.   29. (Tu) sei troppo fastidiosa.   30. Allora, che cosa aspetti?   31. Va bene, ci provo.   32. Questa donna qui è proprio bella.   33. Quella donna è senz'altro sposata, perché porta l'anello.   34. Forse la donna è un po' timida.   35. Non ci credo, perché lei è sempre sicura di sé.

4·2   1. (Lui) capisce molto.   2. (Noi) finiamo alle cinque e poi andiamo da Maria/alla casa di Maria.   3. Il fratello di Maria dorme fino a mezzogiorno.   4. capiscono   5. dormono   6. finiscono   7. capisci

8. il mio amico; i miei amici   9. tua zia; le tue zie (*With family and relatives the article is dropped only in the singular, not the plural.*)   10. tuo zio; i tuoi zii   11. la sua amica; le sue amiche (*Recall that* **suo** *translates as both "his" and "her," but the form must agree with the noun.*)   12. la sua amica; le sue amiche (*Same as above.*)   13. nostro padre; i nostri padri   14. il nostro professore; i nostri professori   15. vostro fratello; i vostri fratelli   16. la Sua casa; le Sue case   17. la loro zia; le loro zie (*Recall that the exception to the article being dropped is* **loro**.)   18. il loro amico; i loro amici.   19. Mio fratello è noioso, ma è assai carino.   20. (Io) trovo la mia amica simpatica e vivace.   21. (Io) non conosco l'amico di mio fratello.   22. Il fratello della mia amica sembra un ragazzo sincero e educato.   23. Capisco!   24. (Tu) sei innamorata?   25. (Tu) sei innamorato?   26. (Voi) siete tutti e due innamorati?   27. Mi piacciono i ragazzi felici e ottimisti.   28. Mi piacciono anche le ragazze felici e ottimiste. (*Remember that the plural of an adjective ending in* -e, *like* **felice**, *is* -i, *even in the feminine.*)

4·3   1. Vorrei degli anelli.   2. Vorrei dei cellulari.   3. Vorrei dei francobolli.   4. Vorrei dei libri.   5. Vorrei dei panini.   6. la sua moglie bella   7. il suo fratello carino   8. il loro figlio grande   9. la loro figlia alta   10. il nostro nonno simpatico   11. la tua mamma vivace   12. il mio papà educato   13. il suo marito bello   14. la nostra cugina piccola/la nostra piccola cugina   15. il loro cugino basso   16. Alessandro, mi presti dei soldi?   17. (Io) non posso.   18. Sei proprio come il papà!   19. Sei proprio come la mamma!   20. Perché non chiedi al nonno o alla nonna?   21. Hai ragione e sei molto generosa.   22. La nostra piccola cugina è nata ieri?   23. (Lei) assomiglia a sua madre.   24. Tutta la mia famiglia è simpatica.

5   Jobs and homes

5·1   1. i buoni zii (*Don't forget to change the article form* **gli** *to fit before* **buoni**, *not* **zii**.)   2. le belle ragazze   3. la bella signora   4. la bell'amica   5. i begli amici   6. il bell'uomo   7. il buon uomo   8. il bello zio   9. il buon panino   10. qualche amica   11. degli studenti   12. qualche cornetto   13. dei libri   14. Marco, parla italiano! (**tu**-*form*)   15. Signor Verdi, parli italiano! (**Lei**-*form*)   16. Giovanni e Maria, aspettate qui! (**voi**-*form*)   17. Signorine, aspettino qui! (**Loro**-*form*)   18. Conosci un bravo avvocato o un bravo dentista?   19. Hai mal di denti?   20. Voglio diventare un medico o forse un architetto.   21. (È) impossibile.   22. È forse meglio fare qualcosa di più pratico?   23. Secondo me, tu sei nato per essere un insegnante.   24. (Io) preferisco fare il meccanico/essere un meccanico piuttosto che (un) impiegato (-a).   25. Fa' quello che vuoi!

5·2   1. hai aspettato   2. ha lavorato   3. ha mandato   4. abbiamo prestato   5. avete sbagliato   6. hanno telefonato   7. Maria, leggi il bel romanzo!   8. Signora Verdi, chieda un caffè!   9. Marco e Maria, prendete un po' di caffè!   10. Signori, leggano il nuovo libro.   11. (Scusi), cerco (un) lavoro nella Sua ditta.   12. Non ho mai lavorato in una ditta di informatica.   13. (Io) ho una laurea in matematica.   14. (Io) ho creato diversi programmi all'università.   15. (Io) ho qualche esperienza di lavoro.   16. (Io) ho lavorato per una banca diversi anni fa.   17. Torni la prossima settimana per un'intervista ufficiale.   18. Eccomi di nuovo.   19. Quanti anni ha?   20. (Io) voglio fare/Le faccio una serie di domande.   21. Qual è il Suo indirizzo?   22. Abito/Vivo in centro.   23. Qual è il Suo stato civile?   24. Mi piacciono quei bei programmi.   25. Cerchi la banca?

5·3   1. Giovanni, dormi!   2. Signora Verdi, dorma!   3. Marco e Maria, finite il caffè!   4. Signorine, finiscano il libro!   5. Bruna, finisci il cornetto!   6. Signora Verdi, finisca il panino!   7. Marco e Maria, dormite fino a tardi!   8. Questa casa è molto piccola, ma ha una bella cucina, una bella camera, e un bagno grande.   9. La casa ha un salotto magnifico e una sala da pranzo eccezionale.   10. Il garage, però, è molto piccolo.   11. L'entrata è assai grande.   12. (Io) devo comprare tanti nuovi mobili.   13. (Io) ho già un bel divano e una bella poltrona.   14. (Io) voglio comprare un nuovo frigorifero, un nuovo letto per la camera e un nuovo tavolo.   15. Conviene rimanere nel mio condominio.

6   Daily life

6·1   1. Vorrei delle fragole.   2. Vorrei dei piselli.   3. Vorrei delle pere.   4. Vorrei delle pesche.   5. Vorrei dei fagioli.   6. Vorrei del formaggio.   7. Vorrei del prosciutto.   8. Vorrei della carne.   9. Vorrei del pesce.   10. Vorrei del pane.   11. Vorrei dell'acqua.   12. Vorrei del latte.   13. Vorrei del vino.   14. Vorrei della frutta.   15. Vorrei della verdura.   16. Maria, non tornare domani!   17. Signor Marchi, non faccia questo!   18. Marco, non fare quella domanda al professore!   19. Giovanni e Bruna, non siate vivaci!   20. Maria, non avere fretta! (*Maria, don't be in a hurry!*)   21. Quante fragole desidera?   22. Vorrei una dozzina di mele e un chilo di pesche.   23. Queste fragole sono più fresche.   24. Basta così.   25. Desidera?   26. Vorrei una dozzina di fette di prosciutto.   27. Vorrei anche un po' di salame. (*Note the spelling in*

Italian.)   28. Il formaggio è buonissimo/molto buono e freschissimo/molto fresco.   29. Vorrei comprare del prosciutto alla pizzicheria in via Nazionale.   30. Vorrei comprare del pane al panificio in via Dante.

6·2   1. Professor Giusto, vada in centro!   2. Marco e Bruna, andate in centro!   3. Maria, di' la verità!
4. Dottoressa Marinelli, dica la verità!   5. Giovanni e Maria, dite la verità!   6. Marco, vieni qui!
7. Signora Martini, venga qui!   8. Marco e Maria, venite qui!   9. Ieri ho comprato una camicetta bianca e una cintura gialla.   10. Ieri ho comprato due maglie grigie e una camicia marrone.   11. Ieri ho comprato una cravatta viola, una borsa rossa, un abito verde e una giacca nera.   12. Il professore non ha avuto tempo.
13. (Noi) non abbiamo dovuto comprare quell'abito.   14. (Voi) non avete potuto comprare quegli stivali.
15. (Tu) non hai voluto leggere quel libro.   16. (Io) non ho capito la verità.   17. (Tu) non hai dormito fino a tardi.   18. Il ragazzo non ha preferito il cornetto.   19. (Noi) non abbiamo finito di lavorare.   20. (Voi) non avete capito il libro.   21. Vorrei comprare una giacca alla moda.   22. Che taglia porta?   23. Vuole provarsi un vestito azzurro?   24. Vorrei (dei) pantaloni che vanno insieme con la (colla) giacca verde.
25. Dov'è il camerino?   26. Vada lì, a destra.   27. Quanto costano gli stivali e le scarpe?   28. Le scarpe sono in saldo.   29. Che numero porta?   30. Le stanno proprio bene.

6·3   1. (Io) non sono andato (-a) al supermercato.   2. (Tu) non sei venuto (-a) con loro in centro.   3. Quell'uomo non è tornato dal centro.   4. Quella donna non è tornata dal centro.   5. (Noi) non siamo stati (-e) in Italia.
6. (Voi) non siete venuti (-e) in centro.   7. Gli studenti non sono rimasti in classe.   8. Le donne non sono state al bar.   9. Quegli stivali non sono costati molto.   10. Quelle scarpe non sono costate tanto.   11. Marco non ha chiesto quelle domande al professore. (*Be careful! This verb is conjugated with* **avere**.)   12. Maria non ha detto la verità.   13. (Io) non ho fatto la spesa ieri.   14. Mio fratello non ha letto quel libro.
15. (Io) non ho preso il caffè al bar.   16. (Tu) non hai visto Maria ieri.   17. (Loro) non sono venuti (-e) con noi.   18. Vorrei depositare dei soldi/del denaro nel mio conto.   19. Vorrei prelevare dei soldi/del denaro dal mio altro conto.   20. Firmi questo modulo.   21. Vorrei (dei) biglietti di taglio piccolo.   22. Mi può cambiare questi biglietti in spiccioli?

7   Weather, seasons, and holidays

7·1   1. Il tuo amico non va mai al cinema.   2. La sua amica non sa niente/nulla.   3. Loro non vanno più in montagna.   4. Maria non conosce nessuno.   5. Io non voglio né la carne né il pesce.   6. Maria non ti chiama mai.   7. Maria non ci chiama mai.   8. Maria non vi chiama mai.   9. Maria non lo chiama mai.   10. Maria non la chiama mai.   11. Maria non li chiama mai.   12. Maria non le chiama mai.
13. (Io) non esco mai.   14. Le ragazze sono già uscite/sono uscite già.   15. Marco, esci con Maria!   16. Signora Verdi, esca con Suo marito!   17. Mio fratello è uscito qualche momento fa.   18. Marco, esci spesso?
19. Fa troppo freddo.   20. Fa troppo caldo.   21. Preferisco andare in montagna piuttosto che andare al mare.   22. Nevica sempre d'inverno.   23. Non sei mai contento (-a).   24. Vieni in centro con me.
25. Non voglio andare in centro perché piove forte.   26. Ho voglia di uscire.   27. Andiamo al cinema.

7·2   1. Maria non ti ha parlato.   2. Maria non ci ha parlato.   3. Maria non vi ha parlato.   4. Maria non gli ha parlato.   5. Maria non le ha parlato.   6. Maria non gli ha parlato.   7. Maria non gli ha parlato.   8. Maria è uscita con te.   9. Maria ha parlato a noi.   10. Maria è uscita con voi.   11. Maria ha parlato a lui.
12. Maria è uscita con lei.   13. Maria ha parlato a loro.   14. Maria è uscita con loro.   15. Amo la primavera ma odio l'inverno.   16. Preferisco l'estate perché amo il caldo.   17. A primavera sbocciano le piante.
18. Sei romantico (-a).   19. Il mio amore per te è molto forte.   20. Mi piace la neve.   21. Amo l'autunno perché cadono le foglie.

7·3   1. Io lo ho (l'ho) preso a quel bar.   2. Noi lo abbiamo letto già.   3. Mia sorella le ha comprate ieri.
4. La sua amica la ha (l'ha) fatta ieri.   5. Mia cugina non li ha voluti.   6. Non lo ho (l'ho) ancora finito.
7. Maria non la ha (l'ha) mai detta.   8. Li ho finiti.   9. Non le ho mai preferite.   10. Io te li ho comprati.
11. Mio fratello gliele ha chieste ieri.   12. Mio fratello glieli ha comprati ieri. (*Note that* **le** + **li** *becomes* **glieli**.)   13. Tu ce li hai mandati, vero?   14. Io ve lo ho preso, va bene?   15. È già Natale!   16. Amo le feste natalizie.   17. Non mi piace la Pasqua perché piove sempre.   18. Amo la primavera perché fa bel tempo e tutto comincia a crescere.   19. Tutti vanno in vacanza in agosto.   20. Purtroppo (io) devo lavorare.   21. Sei un vero amico/una vera amica!

8   Leisure time

8·1   1. Giovanni, comprali!   2. Maria, non prenderli!   3. Signor Mazzini, mi chiami!   4. Claudia, chiamami!
5. Marco e Maria, parlategli!   6. Finiamola!   7. Signora Brunello, ci parli!   8. Io leggevo molti libri.
9. Tu rimanevi sempre in casa.   10. Mio fratello credeva molte cose.   11. Mia sorella usciva spesso.

12. Noi venivamo spesso in Italia.   13. Voi vedevate mia cugina spesso.   14. Loro capivano molto.   15. Io sapevo tante cose.   16. Tu non potevi mai uscire.   17. Lui finiva di lavorare presto.   18. Noi dormivamo fino a tardi.   19. Ti piace sciare?   20. Preferisci il nuoto o il tennis?   21. C'è una piscina qui vicino.   22. Non posso andare in palestra perché c'è il campionato di calcio alla TV/in TV.   23. Vado da solo (-a).   24. Ti piace la pallacanesto e l'automobilismo?   25. Pratichi il pugilato, l'atletica leggera, la lotta o il pattinaggio?   26. Preferisco fare il footing.   27. Non ho un buon partner.

8·2   1. Lui era sposato due anni fa quando l'ho conosciuto.   2. Marco stava bene ieri.   3. In Italia faceva caldo l'estate scorsa.   4. Io dicevo sempre la verità quando ero bambino.   5. Noi dicevamo sempre la verità quando eravamo bambini.   6. Anche voi dicevate sempre la verità quando eravate bambini.   7. Tu dicevi sempre tutto a tua madre.   8. Anche mia sorella diceva sempre tutto a sua madre.   9. Loro non dicevano mai la verità quando erano bambini.   10. Io non stavo bene ieri.   11. Anche loro non stavano bene ieri.   12. Io facevo molte cose quando ero bambino.   13. Maria sta andando in centro.   14. Io sto leggendo un bel romanzo.   15. Tu stai dicendo la verità.   16. Sta facendo bel tempo.   17. Noi stavamo guardando la televisione ieri sera.   18. Voi stavate parlando al professore.   19. I miei amici stavano uscendo quando hai chiamato.   20. Io stavo dormendo quando hai chiamato.   21. Non mi piace né la musica classica né la musica moderna.   22. Dove vuoi uscire?   23. Vorrei andare a ballare o a un locale notturno.   24. Mi annoio sempre.   25. Vuoi andare a una discoteca?   26. Vuoi andare invece al teatro?   27. Preferisco stare/rimanere a casa a guardare la televisione.

8·3   1. quarto   2. quinti   3. sesta   4. settime   5. ottavo   6. nona   7. decima   8. quarantacinquesimo (*Recall that* **programma** *is masculine.*)   9. sessantreesima   10. bevi   11. beve   12. beviamo   13. bevete   14. bevono   15. (Io) bevevo il latte quando ero bambino (-a).   16. Anche loro bevevano il latte quando erano bambini (-e).   17. Marco, bevi tutta l'acqua!   18. (Loro) hanno bevuto già tutto il caffè.   19. vivacemente   20. assolutamente   21. precisamente   22. eccezionalmente   23. Cosa prendono?   24. Per primo piatto, prendo le lasagne, piuttosto che il minestrone.   25. Ho cambiato idea. Prendo invece gli gnocchi.   26. Per secondo piatto, vorrei mangiare una cotoletta di vitello con contorno di patatine, ma non posso, e allora prendo la trota alla griglia con contorno di verdure.   27. Da bere prendo una bottiglia di vino bianco e una bottiglia di acqua minerale.   28. (Cameriere/Cameriera), posso avere un cucchiaio, una coltello e una forchetta (per favore)?   29. (Cameriere/Cameriera), posso avere un bicchiere nuovo e un tovagliolo?   30. Dov'è la tazza?   31. (Cameriere/Cameriera), posso avere il menù?   32. (Noi) non abbiamo una prenotazione.   33. Non voglio l'antipasto.   34. (Cameriere/Cameriera), mi può portare il conto (per favore)?   35. Non devo lasciare una mancia.   36. Vorrei della frutta e del formaggio.   37. Ho cambiato idea. Preferisco il gelato al cioccolato.   38. Vorrei un caffè lungo, non un macchiato.

9 Traveling

9·1   1. arriverà   2. parleremo   3. pagheremo   4. mangerete   5. comincerò   6. cercherai   7. chiederai   8. crederò   9. prenderemo   10. pioverà   11. leggeranno   12. capirò   13. finiranno   14. partiremo   15. dormirete   16. uscirà   17. Vorrei fare il/un biglietto di andata e ritorno per Roma.   18. Vorrei un biglietto di prima classe.   19. Il treno partirà dal binario numero dodici.   20. (Io) arriverò alla stazione in orario.   21. Il mio amico/La mia amica arriverà in anticipo di qualche minuto.   22. La partenza dell'autobus è alle quattordici e l'arrivo è alle diciassette.   23. (Io) ho ancora tempo.   24. C'è un'edicola qui vicino?

9·2   1. diamo   2. do   3. dai   4. dà   5. date   6. danno   7. (Io) ho dato quelle scarpe a mio fratello.   8. (Tu) davi molte cose a tua sorella.   9. (Lui) mi darà dei soldi/del denaro per uscire stasera.   10. Loro mi darebbero dei soldi/del denaro, ma non possono.   11. lui mangerebbe   12. io cercherei   13. noi partiremmo   14. tu verresti   15. voi sapreste   16. io pagherei   17. tu saresti   18. lei avrebbe   19. io vorrei   20. loro direbbero   21. io farei   22. Non ho fatto la prenotazione.   23. Vorrei una camera che dà sulla piazza.   24. Vorrei una camera singola, non una camera doppia.   25. A quanto viene a/per notte?   26. Potrei avere due chiavi?   27. L'ascensore non funziona.   28. Potrei avere una camera al sesto piano?   29. Dov'è l'atrio?   30. L'uscita è qui.   31. Dov'è l'entrata dell'albergo?   32. Non tornerò mai più in quest'albergo.   33. La colazione non è quasi mai buona.   34. La mia camera è sporca.   35. Vorrei uno sconto.

9·3   1. Eccolo.   2. Eccoli.   3. Eccole.   4. Eccola.   5. Ne prendo.   6. Ne ho mangiati.   7. Ci vado domani.   8. Ci andrò nel pomeriggio.   9. Si deve dire sempre la verità.   10. Si comprano quelle cose in centro.   11. Ecco il mio biglietto.   12. Il volo partirà tra/fra mezz'ora.   13. Meno male!   14. Ecco la Sua (*pol.*)/la tua (*fam.*) carta d'imbarco.   15. Dov'è l'uscita?   16. È laggiù, davanti a quel segnale.   17. Vorrei un posto al finestrino, non al corridoio.   18. Signore e signori, siete pregati di allacciare la cintura/le cinture di sicurezza.   19. Il decollo è previsto tra/fra qualche minuto.   20. Il comandante e l'intero equipaggio vi augurano un buon viaggio.

10   This and that

10·1   1. Tu ti lavi in questo momento.   2. Lui si mette una giacca nuova.   3. Lei si diverte al cinema.   4. Noi ci annoiamo in centro.   5. Voi vi provate diversi tipi di scarpe.   6. Loro si divertono in Italia.   7. Tu ti lavavi ieri.   8. Lui si metteva una giacca nuova.   9. Lei si divertiva al cinema.   10. Noi ci annoiavamo in centro.   11. Voi vi provavate diversi tipi di scarpe.   12. Loro si divertivano in Italia.   13. Tu ti sei lavato (-a) ieri.   14. Lui si è messo una giacca nuova.   15. Lei si è divertita al cinema.   16. Noi ci siamo annoiati (-e) in centro.   17. Voi vi siete provati (-e) diversi tipi di scarpe.   18. Loro si sono divertiti (-e) in Italia.   19. Tu ti laveresti e infatti ti laverai oggi.   20. Lui si metterebbe e infatti si metterà una giacca nuova.   21. Lei si divertirebbe e infatti si divertirà al cinema.   22. Noi ci annoieremmo e infatti ci annoieremo in centro.   23. Voi vi provereste e infatti vi proverete diversi tipi di scarpe.   24. Loro si divertirebbero e infatti si divertiranno in Italia.   25. Che tipo di macchina vorrebbe noleggiare?   26. Posso vedere la Sua patente e (la Sua) carta di credito?   27. Qual è il prezzo?   28. Il prezzo è solo cento euro al/per giorno.   29. Firmi qui.   30. I freni non funzionano.   31. Il volante, l'acceleratore, i fari e il clacson sono nuovi.   32. Gli sportelli e i finestrini sono molto moderni.   33. (Faccia) il pieno, per favore.   34. Dovrei, dopo, controllare l'olio e l'aria nelle gomme, e pulire il parabrezza.

10·2   1. Marco, calmati!   2. Maria, non annoiarti!   3. Signor Verdi, si metta la/una cravatta!   4. Signora Marchi, si provi questi stivali!   5. Bruna, divertiti con mio fratello!   6. Mi piacciono le patatine.   7. Mio fratello piace a Maria.   8. Lui ci piace./Lui piace a noi.   9. Mi piacevano le patatine molti anni fa.   10. Tuo fratello piacerà a Maria.   11. Lui non ci è piaciuto./Lui non è piaciuto a noi.   12. Hai finito di studiare?   13. Macché! Sono stufo (-a) di studiare.   14. Non ce la faccio più!   15. Ti amo con tutto il cuore.   16. Sei il mio vero amore.   17. Ti voglio un mondo di bene.   18. Sono veramente fortunato (-a).

10·3   1. Sara è più brava di Maria.   2. Quella donna è meno simpatica di quell'uomo.   3. La dottoressa è più intelligente del professore.   4. I nostri amici sono più sinceri di quegli studenti.   5. Maria è più amichevole che brava.   6. Quell'uomo è più generoso che simpatico.   7. Il professore è più vivace che intelligente.   8. Quegli studenti sono più timidi che sinceri.   9. Hai sentito quello che ha fatto Antonio?   10. Qualcuno mi ha detto che si è divorziato./Mi hanno detto che si è divorziato.   11. Sta andando con un'altra donna.   12. Mascalzone!   13. La sua povera moglie è così brava.   14. Maria mi ha detto che non aveva denaro.   15. Lei dice troppe bugie.   16. Come molta gente.

Overall review   1. Buongiorno, signorina Marchi.   2. Ciao, Giovanni! Come stai?   3. Mi chiamo Marco Signori.   4. Piacere di conoscerti!   5. Scusi, mi può aiutare?   6. Mi piace molto/tanto quel romanzo.   7. Vorrei un (caffè) espresso, per favore.   8. Quanto costano?   9. Sono le quattordici e venti.   10. A che ora finisce il programma?   11. Quanti anni hai?   12. (Io) sono nato (-a) nel 1995.   13. (Io) abito in via Nazionale, numero 46.   14. (Io) abito a Perugia, proprio nel centro.   15. Mi sa dire dov'è via Boccaccio?   16. (Lei) deve andare a sinistra, non a destra.   17. Pronto. Chi parla?   18. Mi devi mandare un messaggino/un SMS col tuo cellulare.   19. Non mi piacciono gli uomini biondi.   20. Guarda che bella donna!   21. Mio fratello è simpatico e intelligente.   22. La mia amica è molto simpatica.   23. Alessandro è proprio come suo padre/papà.   24. (Lui) è molto carino.   25. Ho mal di denti. Conosci un bravo/una brava dentista?   26. (Io) non voglio fare l'insegnante.   27. (Scusi), cerco un lavoro nella Sua ditta.   28. Qual è il Suo stato civile?   29. Questa casa è molto piccola.   30. (Io) ho bisogno di/devo comprare dei mobili nuovi.   31. Vorrei anche dei piselli e dei fagioli freschi.   32. Vorrei anche del formaggio buonissimo/molto buono.   33. Vorrebbe provarsi questa giacca marrone?   34. Quanto costano questi stivali?   35. Vorrei depositare questi soldi/questo denaro nel mio conto.   36. Vorrei cambiare questi biglietti in spiccioli.   37. Ieri faceva veramente/proprio troppo freddo!   38. Domani (io) vorrei andare in centro.   39. Mio fratello è uscito con Bruna.   40. In autunno cadono le foglie.   41. (Io) amo le feste natalizie.   42. (Io) preferisco quelle scarpe. Allora le prenderò.   43. Marco, non andare in centro perché sta piovendo/piove.   44. Quando (io) ero bambino (-a), andavo spesso al cinema.   45. Cameriere (-a), per primo piatto preferisco il minestrone.   46. Il treno parte dal binario numero sei.   47. La colazione non è mai buona in questo/quest' albergo.   48. Il decollo è previsto tra/fra qualche minuto.   49. Vorrei noleggiare una macchina piccola.   50. (Lui) è un mascalzone. Sta andando con un'altra donna.